# PEOPLE'S REPUBLIC OF CHINA POVERTY REDUCTION AND REGIONAL COOPERATION FUND

## ANNUAL REPORT 2019

**ADB**

ASIAN DEVELOPMENT BANK

# Contents

# Figures and Boxes

# Abbreviations

| | |
|---|---|
| ADB | Asian Development Bank |
| AMF | Accountability Mechanism Framework |
| APEC | Asia-Pacific Economic Cooperation |
| ASEAN | Association of Southeast Asian Nations |
| ASEAN+3 | ASEAN plus Japan, the People's Republic of China, and the Republic of Korea |
| BIMP-EAGA | Brunei Darussalam–Indonesia–Malaysia–Philippines East ASEAN Growth Area |
| BRI | Belt and Road Initiative |
| CAREC | Central Asia Regional Economic Cooperation |
| CTTDF | CAREC Think Tanks Development Forum |
| CWRD | Central and West Asia Department |
| DMC | developing member country |
| EARD | East Asia Department |
| ECD | economic corridor development |
| ERCD | Economic Research and Regional Cooperation Department |
| GMS | Greater Mekong Subregion |
| IED | Independent Evaluation Department |
| IMT-GT | Indonesia–Malaysia–Thailand Growth Triangle |
| Lao PDR | Lao People's Democratic Republic |
| MOF | Ministry of Finance, PRC |
| NPL | nonperforming loan |
| OCO | Office of Cofinancing Operations |
| OCRP | Office of the Compliance Review Panel |
| PARD | Pacific Department |
| PRC | People's Republic of China |
| PRC Fund | People's Republic of China Poverty Reduction and Regional Cooperation Fund |
| RCI | regional cooperation and integration |
| RKSI | (ADB–PRC) Regional Knowledge Sharing Initiative |
| SARD | South Asia Department |
| SDCC | Sustainable Development and Climate Change Department |
| SDPF | Partner Funds Division, SDCC |
| SERD | Southeast Asia Department |
| SEZ | special economic zone |
| SPS | sanitary and phytosanitary |
| TA | technical assistance |
| TCR | technical assistance completion report |
| TRTA | transaction technical assistance |
| WTO | World Trade Organization |

# Executive Summary

The People's Republic of China Poverty Reduction and Regional Cooperation Fund (PRC Fund) is the first trust fund established by an Asian Development Bank (ADB) developing member country (DMC). After an initial contribution of $20.0 million from the Government of the PRC in 2005, the Fund was replenished with $20.0 million in March 2012 and $50.0 million in July 2017, increasing the PRC's total contribution to $90.0 million. The Fund is aimed at supporting poverty reduction, regional cooperation and integration (RCI), and knowledge sharing through technical assistance (TA) and grants that explore and benefit from synergies among the Belt and Road Initiative (BRI), Central Asia Regional Economic Cooperation (CAREC), and the Greater Mekong Subregion (GMS) programs, and other RCI initiatives. Within ADB, the Sustainable Development and Climate Change Department (SDCC) manages the Fund.

Since its inception in March 2005, the PRC Fund has approved 115 applications representing 106 TA and grants with a total cost of $58.14 million. Of the 115 approved applications, 112 totaling $56.39 million were approved between 2005 and 2019 by the PRC Ministry of Finance (MOF) and 3 others worth $1.75 million were approved in the first 3 months of 2020.[*] Public sector management, industry and trade, energy, and water and other urban infrastructure and services have been among the sectors covered.

In 2019, 10 projects totaling $7.3 million were approved: three transaction technical assistance (TRTA) totaling $4.1 million, one grant worth $0.75 million, and six knowledge and support TA projects worth $2.45 million. These involve the provision of policy advice and capacity-building services in energy; transport; industry and trade; water and other urban infrastructure and services; public sector management; agriculture, natural resources, and rural development; and finance in ADB DMCs. The volume of approved applications in 2019 marked another high point in annual approvals representing continuous growth since the Fund's establishment.

As of 31 December 2019, ADB had approved 103 projects after the PRC MOF's approval. Of this total, 66 projects (64%) have financially closed, 35 (34%) remain active, and 2 have elapsed. Fifty-eight of the 66 completed projects have TA completion ratings of *highly successful* (16%) or *successful* (72%), for an overall success rate of 88%.

In 2019, the PRC Fund prioritized support for TRTA, particularly project preparation to better meet the requirements of ADB's Strategy 2030 and establish closer links with ADB's main operations. In fact, the PRC MOF has approved three TRTA projects totaling $4.1 million to support sectors such as water and other urban infrastructure and services, and energy.

---

[*] The three projects approved by the PRC MOF in 2020 were under the 2019 Batch 3 application. Note that the number of projects and corresponding amount refer to applications approved by the PRC MOF within the specified year.

# PRC Fund at a Glance

**1**st **TRUST FUND**
Established by an
ADB DMC

**2** **TYPES OF SUPPORT**
Technical assistance
Grant

**3** **PILLARS**
Poverty reduction
Regional cooperation
Knowledge sharing

**$90** million
Total Contribution

**15**
Years of Support

**115**
Approved
Applications

ADB = Asian Development Bank, DMC = developing member country, PRC Fund = People's Republic of China Poverty Reduction and
Regional Cooperation Fund.
Source: ADB database.

## Operational Highlights, 2015–2019
($ million)

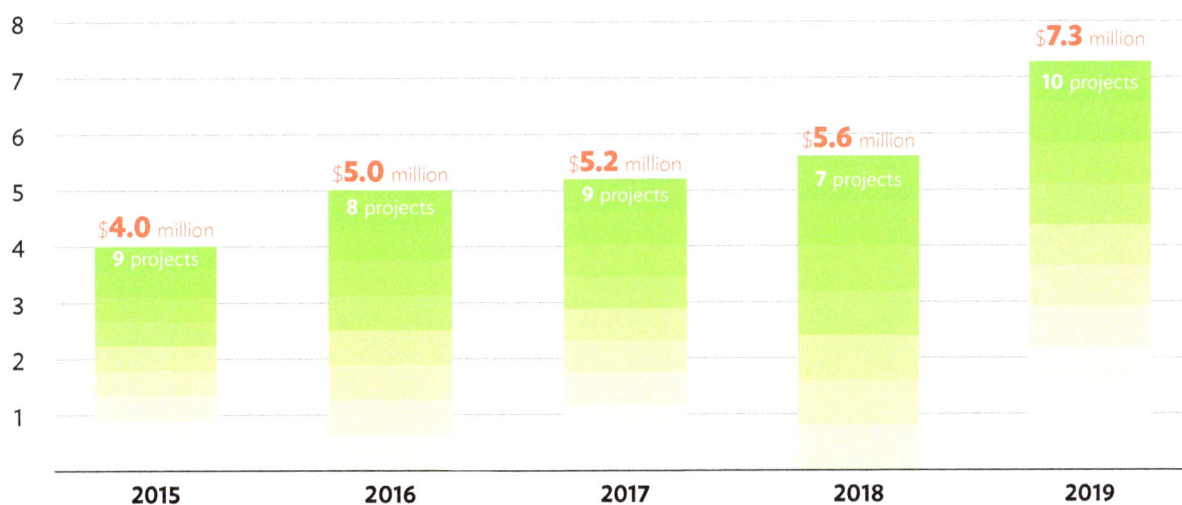

| Year | Amount | Projects |
| --- | --- | --- |
| 2015 | $4.0 million | 9 projects |
| 2016 | $5.0 million | 8 projects |
| 2017 | $5.2 million | 9 projects |
| 2018 | $5.6 million | 7 projects |
| 2019 | $7.3 million | 10 projects |

Note: The number of projects and corresponding amounts refer to applications approved by the People's Republic of China Ministry of
Finance within the specified year.
Source: ADB database.

# 2019 Approvals

| Approved Applications | Transaction Technical Assistance | Knowledge and Support Technical Assistance | Grant |
|---|---|---|---|
| **10** | **$4.1** million | **$2.45** million | **$0.75** million |

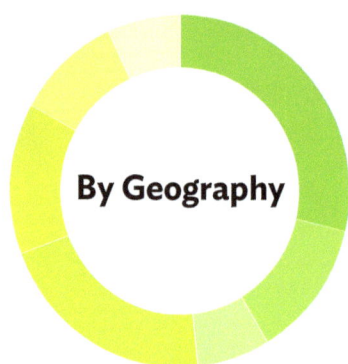

## By Geography

**49%** REGIONAL

- **29%** CAREC $2.1 million
- **13%** Other $1.0 million
- **7%** GMS $0.5 million

**51%** COUNTRY-SPECIFIC

- **21%** Pakistan $1.5 million
- **14%** Uzbekistan $1.0 million
- **10%** Bangladesh $0.8 million
- **7%** Mongolia $0.5 million

## By Sector

- **39%** Energy $2.9 million
- **34%** Water and Other Urban Infrastructure and Services $2.5 million
- **7%** Industry and Trade $0.5 million
- **7%** Transport $0.5 million
- **7%** Public Sector Management $0.5 million
- **3%** Agriculture, Natural Resources, and Rural Development $0.2 million
- **3%** Finance $0.2 million

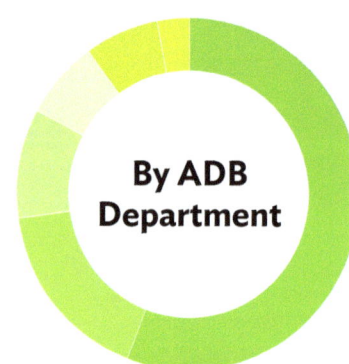

## By ADB Department

- **56%** CWRD $4.1 million
- **17%** EARD $1.2 million
- **10%** SARD $0.8 million
- **7%** SERD $0.5 million
- **7%** SDCC $0.5 million
- **3%** OCRP $0.2 million

ADB = Asian Development Bank; CAREC = Central Asia Regional Economic Cooperation; CWRD = Central and West Asia Department; EARD = East Asia Department; GMS = Greater Mekong Subregion; OCRP = Office of the Compliance Review Panel, ADB; SARD = South Asia Department; SDCC = Sustainable Development and Climate Change Department; SERD = Southeast Asia Department.
Notes: 1. "Other" refers to projects that involve countries in only one region or from two or more regions.
2. Percentages may not total 100% because of rounding.
Source: ADB database.

# ADB's Strategy 2030: Seven Operational Priorities

The seven approved applications in 2019 are closely aligned with ADB's seven operational priorities, as stated in Strategy 2030.

| 2019 Approvals | | Strategy 2030: Seven Operational Priorities | | | | | | |
|---|---|:---:|:---:|:---:|:---:|:---:|:---:|:---:|
| Project Number | Project Title | 👤 | ⚢ | 🍃 | 🏙 | 🌾 | 🏛 | ✹ |
| Grant 0675-BAN | Dhaka and Western Zone Transmission Grid Expansion Project | | ✓ | ✓ | ✓ | | ✓ | ✓ |
| TA 9718-REG | Developing an Accountability Mechanism Framework for Financial Intermediaries | | | | | | ✓ | ✓ |
| TA 9824-REG | Better Customs for Better Client Services in Central Asia Regional Economic Cooperation Countries | | ✓ | | | | ✓ | ✓ |
| TA 9938-MON | Methane Gas Supply Chain Development Master Plan | ✓ | | | | | ✓ | |
| TA 9715-UZB | Preparing Urban Development and Improvement Projects | ✓ | ✓ | ✓ | ✓ | | ✓ | |
| TA 9792-REG | Preparing Sustainable Energy Projects In Central Asia | ✓ | | ✓ | | | ✓ | |
| TA 9839-PAK | Preparing Urban Development Projects | ✓ | ✓ | ✓ | ✓ | | ✓ | ✓ |
| TA 9791-REG | Strengthening Fiscal Governance and Sustainability in Public–Private Partnerships | ✓ | | ✓ | ✓ | | ✓ | |
| TA 9918-REG | Connecting the Railways of the Greater Mekong Subregion (Phase 2) | | | | | | ✓ | ✓ |
| TA 9846-REG | Developing Partnerships for Knowledge Sharing on Natural Capital Investment in the Yangtze River Economic Belt | ✓ | | ✓ | | ✓ | ✓ | |

ADB = Asian Development Bank, BAN = Bangladesh, MON = Mongolia, PAK = Pakistan, REG = regional, TA = technical assistance, UZB = Uzbekistan.
Sources: ADB database; ADB Strategy 2030: Achieving a Prosperous, Inclusive, Resilient, and Sustainable Asia and the Pacific.

## Strategy 2030's Seven Operational Priorities

| Addressing remaining poverty and reducing inequalities | Accelerating progress in gender equality | Tackling climate change, building climate and disaster resilience, and enhancing environmental sustainability | Making cities more livable | Promoting rural development and food security | Strengthening governance and institutional capacity | Fostering regional cooperation and integration |
|---|---|---|---|---|---|---|

# Cumulative Portfolio, 2005–2019

**Approved Applications**

# 115

**Technical Assistance**

# $58.14 million

Note: Of the 115 approved applications, 112 totaling $56.39 million were approved between 2005 and 2019 by the People's Republic of China Ministry of Finance and 3 others worth $1.75 million were approved in January 2020.

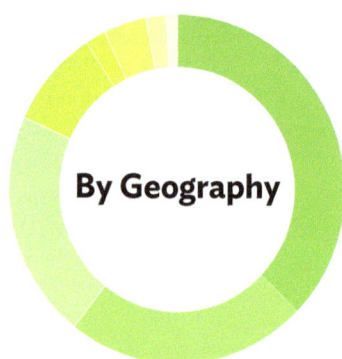

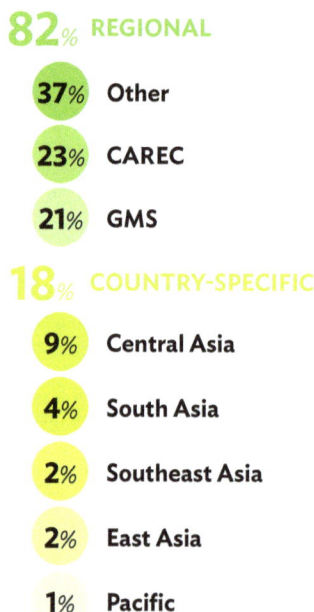

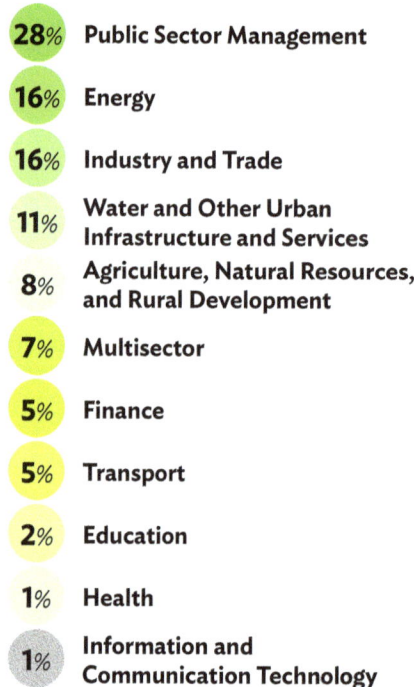

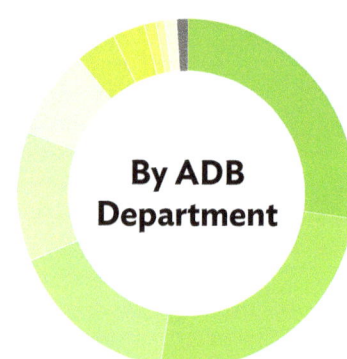

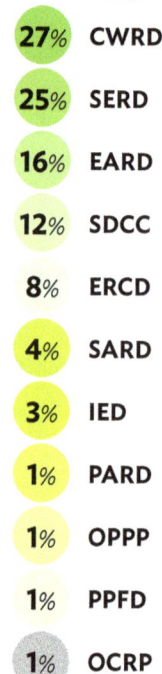

## By Geography

**82% REGIONAL**

- **37%** Other
- **23%** CAREC
- **21%** GMS

**18% COUNTRY-SPECIFIC**

- **9%** Central Asia
- **4%** South Asia
- **2%** Southeast Asia
- **2%** East Asia
- **1%** Pacific

## By Sector

- **28%** Public Sector Management
- **16%** Energy
- **16%** Industry and Trade
- **11%** Water and Other Urban Infrastructure and Services
- **8%** Agriculture, Natural Resources, and Rural Development
- **7%** Multisector
- **5%** Finance
- **5%** Transport
- **2%** Education
- **1%** Health
- **1%** Information and Communication Technology

## By ADB Department

- **27%** CWRD
- **25%** SERD
- **16%** EARD
- **12%** SDCC
- **8%** ERCD
- **4%** SARD
- **3%** IED
- **1%** PARD
- **1%** OPPP
- **1%** PPFD
- **1%** OCRP

ADB = Asian Development Bank; CAREC = Central Asia Regional Economic Cooperation; CWRD = Central and West Asia Department; EARD = East Asia Department; ERCD = Economic Research and Regional Cooperation Department; GMS = Greater Mekong Subregion; IED = Independent Evaluation Department; OCRP = Office of the Compliance Review Panel; OPPP = Office of Public–Private Partnership; PARD = Pacific Department; PPFD = Procurement, Portfolio and Financial Management Department; SARD = South Asia Department, ADB; SDCC = Sustainable Development and Climate Change Department; SERD = Southeast Asia Department.

Notes: 1. "Other" refers to projects that involve countries in only one region or from two or more regions.
2. Percentages may not total 100% because of rounding.
Source: ADB database.

# Chapter 1

# Background

## Overview

This annual report of the People's Republic of China Poverty Reduction and Regional Cooperation Fund (PRC Fund) for 2019 covers the period from 1 January to 31 December. It presents the background and objectives, project activities, and achievements of the Fund. Established in March 2005, the PRC Fund provides technical assistance (TA) and grants to developing member countries (DMCs)[1] of the Asian Development Bank (ADB) for economic and social development.

## Objectives

The PRC Fund aims to contribute to poverty reduction, regional cooperation and knowledge sharing, and economic and social development in ADB's DMCs in an accelerated manner and with tangible results. It does so by providing TA and grants that promote ADB's overarching goal of poverty reduction, as well as its Strategy 2030,[2] regional cooperation and integration (RCI) strategy,[3] and knowledge management directions and action plan.[4]

## Eligibility

The Fund supports six types of activities: (i) transaction technical assistance (TRTA), particularly project preparation support; (ii) DMC institutional development and capacity building; (iii) innovative and demonstrative programs and projects; (iv) knowledge sharing, including knowledge products and human resources development; (v) South–South knowledge exchange and dissemination activities between the PRC and other DMCs; and (vi) grants contributing to regional connectivity.

The Fund supports both regional and country-specific activities. For the regional component, efforts to harness synergies between the Belt and Road Initiative (BRI), Greater Mekong Subregion (GMS),[5] and Central Asia Regional Economic Cooperation (CAREC)[6] programs and ADB's RCI strategies and operations have priority. The PRC is not eligible as a sole beneficiary, but it can participate in regional activities supported by the Fund.

---

1   ADB. Members. http://www.adb.org/about/members.
2   ADB. 2018. *Strategy 2030*. Manila.
3   ADB. 2006. *Regional Cooperation and Integration Strategy*. Manila.
4   ADB. 2013. *Knowledge Management Directions and Action Plan (2013–2015): Supporting "Finance ++" at the Asian Development Bank*. Manila.
5   The Greater Mekong Subregion consists of Cambodia, the Lao People's Democratic Republic (Lao PDR), Myanmar, the People's Republic of China (PRC, specifically Yunnan Province and Guangxi Zhuang Autonomous Region), Thailand, and Viet Nam.
6   The CAREC Program is a partnership of 11 countries (Afghanistan, Azerbaijan, Georgia, Kazakhstan, Kyrgyz Republic, Mongolia, Pakistan, the People's Republic of China, Tajikistan, Turkmenistan, and Uzbekistan), supported by six multilateral institutions, working together to promote development through cooperation, leading to accelerated growth and poverty reduction.

# Processing of Technical Assistance and Grant Applications

ADB administers the Fund in accordance with ADB's standard procedures for projects. Within ADB, the Sustainable Development and Climate Change Department (SDCC) acts as the fund manager,[7] managing and coordinating the review and submission of applications and their approval by the PRC Ministry of Finance (MOF).

Project applications should (i) be aligned with ADB's country partnership strategy, country operations business plan (COBP), and regional cooperation partnership strategy; (ii) include discussions with key DMC stakeholders; (iii) disseminate and apply DMC expertise; (iv) encourage contributions, including in kind, from the beneficiary DMCs; and (v) use the Fund in the most cost-effective way.

Project applications are submitted to SDCC three times a year.[8] SDCC does a preliminary review of the applications to ensure compliance with the implementing guidelines and eligibility criteria of the Fund, and prioritizes applications to be submitted to the PRC MOF for funding consideration. The PRC MOF confirms funding decisions on applications. After funding approval, the projects are to be processed following ADB's standard policies, procedures, and guidelines for project approval. Project implementation, supervision, and monitoring are handled by concerned departments and offices following ADB's standard policies and procedures, including consulting services and procurement, social and environmental safeguards, financial management and reporting, anticorruption and governance (Figure 1). To fulfill ADB's fiduciary responsibilities, SDCC coordinates with the related departments and offices in the submission of annual progress reports, a project completion report assessing the performance of completed projects, an evaluation report on the Fund's performance, and the Fund's annual audited financial report.

**Figure 1:** **Approval Process for PRC Fund Technical Assistance and Grant Proposals**

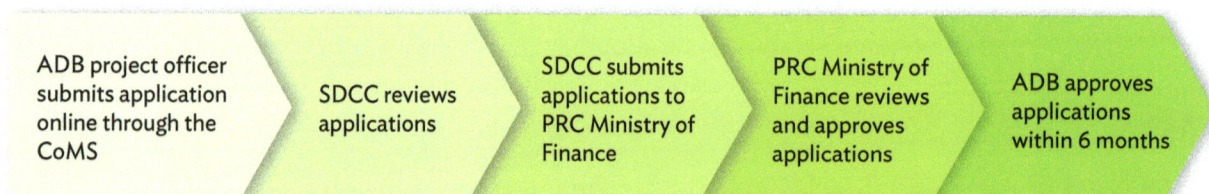

ADB project officer submits application online through the CoMS → SDCC reviews applications → SDCC submits applications to PRC Ministry of Finance → PRC Ministry of Finance reviews and approves applications → ADB approves applications within 6 months

ADB = Asian Development Bank, CoMS = cofinance management system, PRC = People's Republic of China, PRC Fund = People's Republic of China Poverty Reduction and Regional Cooperation Fund, SDCC = Sustainable Development and Climate Change Department.

---

[7] Following its realignment in April 2019, the Office of Cofinancing Operations (OCO) ceased to exist. The administration of the PRC Fund was transferred to a new Partner Funds Division (SDPF) under SDCC.

[8] This process started in January 2018. The deadline set for applications is the end of April for the first batch, the end of July for the second, and the end of November for the third batch. Applications submitted in November are approved the following year.

## Contributions of the Government of the People's Republic of China

The Government of the People's Republic of China made an initial contribution of $20.0 million in March 2005. The first replenishment, amounting to $20.0 million, followed in March 2012, and $50.0 million more was added in July 2017, increasing the PRC's total contribution to $90.0 million.

## Financial Status

As of 31 December 2019, the PRC MOF had approved a total of $53.84 million for 100 TA projects and $2.55 million for three grant projects. The Fund has a balance of $36.27 million, available for future allocation.

# Chapter 2

# Overview of Fund Operations, 2019

## Approvals and Highlights

Ten applications totaling $7.3 million were approved by the PRC MOF in 2019—the highest annual approval volume since the Fund's establishment. Of the 10 approved applications, three are transaction technical assistance (TRTA) totaling $4.1 million, one grant worth $0.75 million, and six knowledge and support TA projects worth $2.45 million. The approved projects were in energy; water and other urban infrastructure and services; industry and trade; transport; public sector management; agriculture, natural resources, and rural development; and finance. Brief summaries of these projects can be found in Figure 2 and Appendix 1.

In October 2018, the PRC MOF broadened the Fund's support to include TRTA, in particular project preparation support to link the Fund more closely with ADB's main operations and deliver tangible results to ADB's DMCs.

**Geographic distribution.** Country-specific projects received the majority of the funding in 2019, with Central Asian countries getting 35% (Pakistan – 21%, Uzbekistan – 14%), followed by Bangladesh (10%) and Mongolia (7%) (Figure 3). Regional[9] projects made up 49% of the total, with CAREC getting 29%, followed by other regional projects (13%) and the GMS (7%).

**Sector distribution.** The Fund approved support for seven sectors in 2019. Among the sectors, energy (39%) had the largest share, followed by water and other urban infrastructure and services (34%); industry and trade, transport, and public sector management (7% each); and agriculture, natural resources, and rural development (3%) and finance (3%) (Figure 4).

**ADB department distribution.** The regional departments received $6.6 million, or around 90% of total Fund approvals in 2019. The most sizable funding support—$4.1 million (56%)—went to the Central and West Asia Department (CWRD). The East Asia Department (EARD) obtained 17%; the South Asia Department (SARD), 10%; and the Southeast Asia Department (SERD), 7%. SDCC received $0.5 million and the Office of the Compliance Review Panel (OCRP) received $0.2 million, or around 10% of total Fund approvals in 2019 (Figure 5).

---

9    Regional projects are projects that fall exclusively under CAREC or the GMS, or under a mix of various regions and subregional programs (e.g., CAREC and Asia-Pacific Economic Cooperation, or APEC; The GMS and the Association of Southeast Asian Nations plus Japan, the People's Republic of China, and the Republic of Korea [ASEAN+3]).

**Figure 2: Approved Projects in 2019 and Their Alignment with Strategy 2030 Operational Priorities**

| Project Number | Project Title | 🔴 | ⚥ | 🍃 | 🏙 | 🌾 | 🏛 | 🌼 |
|---|---|---|---|---|---|---|---|---|
| Grant 0675-BAN | Dhaka and Western Zone Transmission Grid Expansion Project | | ✓ | ✓ | ✓ | | ✓ | ✓ |
| TA 9718-REG | Developing an Accountability Mechanism Framework for Financial Intermediaries | | | | | | ✓ | ✓ |
| TA 9824-REG | Better Customs for Better Client Services in Central Asia Regional Economic Cooperation Countries | | ✓ | | | | ✓ | ✓ |
| TA 9938-MON | Methane Gas Supply Chain Development Master Plan | ✓ | | | | | ✓ | |
| TA 9715-UZB | Preparing Urban Development and Improvement Projects | ✓ | ✓ | ✓ | ✓ | | ✓ | |
| TA 9792-REG | Preparing Sustainable Energy Projects In Central Asia | ✓ | | ✓ | | | ✓ | |
| TA 9839-PAK | Preparing Urban Development Projects | ✓ | ✓ | ✓ | ✓ | | ✓ | ✓ |
| TA 9791-REG | Strengthening Fiscal Governance and Sustainability in Public–Private Partnerships | ✓ | | ✓ | | | ✓ | |
| TA 9918-REG | Connecting the Railways of the Greater Mekong Subregion (Phase 2) | | | | | | ✓ | ✓ |
| TA 9846-REG | Developing Partnerships for Knowledge Sharing on Natural Capital Investment in the Yangtze River Economic Belt | ✓ | | ✓ | | ✓ | ✓ | |

ADB = Asian Development Bank, BAN = Bangladesh, MON = Mongolia, PAK = Pakistan, REG = regional, TA = technical assistance, UZB = Uzbekistan.
Sources: ADB database; ADB Strategy 2030: Achieving a Prosperous, Inclusive, Resilient, and Sustainable Asia and the Pacific.

**Strategy 2030's Seven Operational Priorities**

Addressing remaining poverty and reducing inequalities | Accelerating progress in gender equality | Tackling climate change, building climate and disaster resilience, and enhancing environmental sustainability | Making cities more livable | Promoting rural development and food security | Strengthening governance and institutional capacity | Fostering regional cooperation and integration

**Figure 3: Geographic Distribution, 2019**
(% share of total amount)

Regional **49%**
Country-specific **51%**

CAREC = Central Asia Regional Economic Cooperation,
GMS = Greater Mekong Subregion.
Notes:
1. "Other" refers to projects that involve countries in only one region or from two or more regions.
2. Percentages may not total 100% because of rounding.
Source: ADB database.

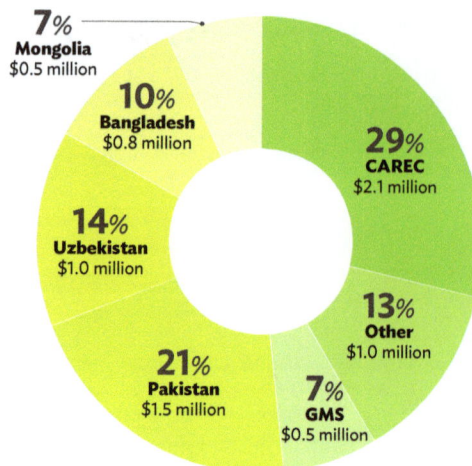

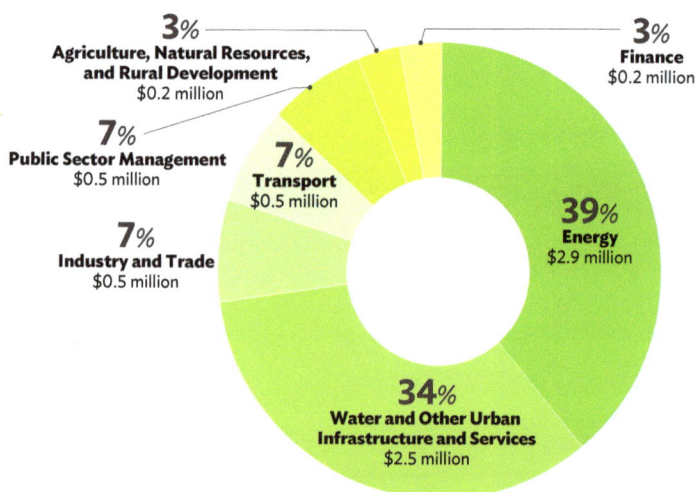

**7%** Mongolia $0.5 million
**10%** Bangladesh $0.8 million
**14%** Uzbekistan $1.0 million
**21%** Pakistan $1.5 million
**29%** CAREC $2.1 million
**13%** Other $1.0 million
**7%** GMS $0.5 million

**Figure 4: Sector Distribution, 2019**
(% share of total amount)

Source: ADB database.

**3%** Agriculture, Natural Resources, and Rural Development $0.2 million
**3%** Finance $0.2 million
**7%** Public Sector Management $0.5 million
**7%** Transport $0.5 million
**7%** Industry and Trade $0.5 million
**39%** Energy $2.9 million
**34%** Water and Other Urban Infrastructure and Services $2.5 million

**Figure 5: ADB Department Distribution, 2019**
(% share of total amount)

ADB = Asian Development Bank, CWRD = Central and West Asia Department, EARD = East Asia Department, OCRP = Office of the Compliance Review Panel, SARD = South Asia Department, SDCC = Sustainable Development and Climate Change Department, SERD = Southeast Asia Department.
Source: ADB database.

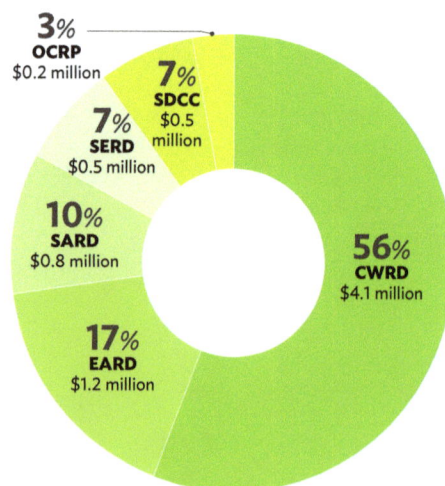

**3%** OCRP $0.2 million
**7%** SDCC $0.5 million
**7%** SERD $0.5 million
**10%** SARD $0.8 million
**17%** EARD $1.2 million
**56%** CWRD $4.1 million

# Project Activities in 2019

This section summarizes project-related activities implemented in 2019 under eight selected active projects supported by the Fund.

## 1 Poverty Reduction

**Regional: Modernizing Sanitary and Phytosanitary Measures to Facilitate Trade**

**Sector:** Industry and Trade
**Amount:** $0.8 million

The regional TA[10] assists Central Asia Regional Economic Cooperation (CAREC) countries in implementing the World Trade Organization (WTO) Agreement on Sanitary and Phytosanitary Measures (SPS) and the CAREC Common Agenda for Modernization of SPS Measures for Trade, which is now part of the CAREC Integrated Trade Agenda 2030. In the second year of its implementation, the TA focused on (i) institutional strengthening for SPS agencies, (ii) regional dialogues to deepen cooperation while promoting coordinated approach to facilitate trade and help countries integrate into regional and global value chains, and (iii) knowledge products.

With TA support, the CAREC SPS Regional Working Group, was established in June 2019 to spearhead policy dialogues and regional cooperation initiatives toward alignment with international standards and good practices on SPS. At the *Policy Dialogue on Regional Pest Surveillance Program* in March 2019, participants agreed on the need to adopt International Plant Protection Convention principles and coordinate pest surveillance and information exchange to reduce trade risks. Participants were also shown how joint quarantine and inspection services are conducted at the border inspection post in Red Bridge between Azerbaijan and Georgia. At the *Policy Dialogue on Regional Program for Control and Prevention of Transboundary Animal Disease* in April 2019, participants agreed on a regional framework to improve animal health situation, and promote international harmonization and coordination to facilitate international trade. Around 93% of the respondents to the post-evaluation surveys reported that the dialogues have improved their understanding of SPS measures, with 100% confirming relevance to their work.

SPS national working groups were also established in 11 CAREC countries to lead SPS modernization through national SPS strategies and action plans. In Turkmenistan, a food safety pilot project was launched in September 2019 to demonstrate the implementation of cost-effective, simplified, risk-based food safety management and inspection systems. It builds capacities in hazard analysis critical control points through trainers' training for inspectors and specialists of the Ministry of Health and Medical Industry and food business operators from dairy, sausage, and confectionery producers and catering services. All the participants reported improvement of their understanding of SPS measures, in general, and that the topics are relevant to their work.

---

10  ADB. Regional: Modernizing Sanitary and Phytosanitary Measures to Facilitate Trade.

The report *Modernizing Sanitary and Phytosanitary Measures in CAREC: An Assessment and the Way Forward*[11] was published in English and Russian in 2019. The study finds that (i) compliance to the WTO SPS Agreement varies across countries and secondary legislation is inadequate; (ii) laboratory facility upgrading and capacity building needs must be addressed; and (iii) SPS border procedures are characterized by unnecessary inspections, causing delays. The report is used as a reference and guide for policy reforms and ongoing research. It offers insights to strengthen risk-based procedures at borders to facilitate movement of agriculture products, which is relevant to ensuring food security in the time of coronavirus disease 2019 (COVID-19). In 2019, advisory and training was provided to Mongolia on risk management to complement the ongoing Regional Upgrades for SPS Measures for Trade project.

> **Training in food safety management and inspection systems.** Inspectors of the State Sanitary and Epidemiological Service of the Ministry of Health undergo practical training in food safety management and inspection systems during the trainers' training in Ashgabat, Turkmenistan in September 2019.

> **CAREC Policy Dialogue on Regional Pest Surveillance Program.** CAREC countries' phytosanitary specialists and inspectors learn international best practices in border inspection and quarantine at the Red Bridge border crossing point between Azerbaijan and Georgia during the program in Tbilisi, Georgia in March 2019.

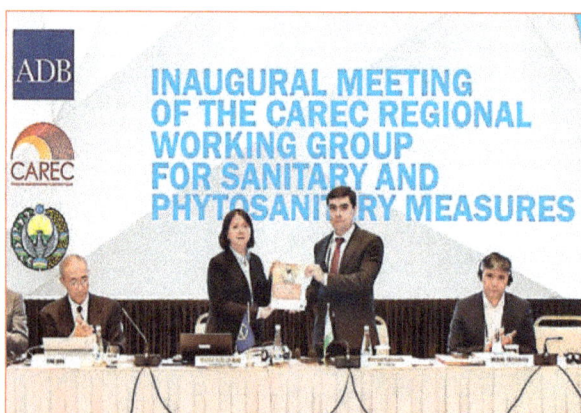

> **Inaugural meeting of the CAREC Regional Working Group for Sanitary and Phytosanitary Measures.** The CAREC SPS Regional Working Group endorsed activities for 2019–2021 and launched the new publication *Modernizing Sanitary and Phytosanitary Measures in CAREC: An Assessment and the Way Forward* at its first meeting in Tashkent, Uzbekistan in June 2019. The assessment covers SPS laws and procedures, laboratory infrastructure, and border services management.

> **CAREC Policy Dialogue on Regional Pest Surveillance Program.** CAREC countries' phytosanitary specialists learn new technologies from a commercial greenhouse producing variety of tomatoes and cucumber in Tbilisi, during the program in Tbilisi, Georgia in March 2019.

---

11  ADB. 2019. *Modernizing Sanitary and Phytosanitary Measures in CAREC: An Assessment and the Way Forward.* Manila. https://www.adb.org/publications/modernizing-sanitary-phytosanitary-measures-carec.

# Regional: Strengthening Institutions for Localizing Agenda 2030 for Sustainable Development

**Sector:** Public Sector Management

**Amount:** $0.5 million

The achievement of the 2030 Agenda and its 17 Sustainable Development Goals (SDGs) will not be possible without the involvement and commitment of the private sector. The 8th National Socio-Economic Development Plan of the Lao People's Democratic Republic (Lao PDR) recognizes this and provides a framework for improving the business friendliness of public policies. The Provincial Facilitation of Investment and Trade Index (ProFIT) gives a voice to the private sector on local economic governance and forges public–private partnership in policy formulation and implementation at the subnational level.

Undertaken since 2018 in collaboration with the Lao National Chamber of Commerce and Industry (LCNNI), ProFIT enables Lao small and medium-sized enterprises (SMEs) to rate their provincial governments on local economic governance issues. Results of the survey are presented and discussed in provincial-level consultations that bring together the business community, subnational governments, and national representatives.

The consultations provide an opportunity for business representatives to engage with government representatives on ways business regulations can be modified to remove unnecessary restrictions, speed up the process of obtaining permits and licenses, and create a business-friendly climate in each province.

Since late 2019, the subproject has supported LCNNI in conducting consultation and survey workshops in 17 provinces in the Lao PDR; this enabled 1,358 Lao SMEs to share their perspectives and complete the survey questionnaire. After compiling the survey results and ranking the provinces according to the perceptions of local business, the subproject will roll out presentations and follow-up consultations in each province.

In 2012, the so-called Sam Sang Directive (or "Three Builds" Directive) requested 15 ministries to delegate more responsibilities, functions, and resources to local administrations, particularly at

> **Consultation meeting and survey workshops in provinces in the Lao People's Democratic Republic.** President of the Lao National Chamber of Commerce and Industry chairs the consultation meeting in the provinces during the data collection process.

district level. Functions to be delegated included public health planning and administration. Health care utilization is low in the Lao PDR, and health-related SDGs remain unfulfilled due to poor quality. Currently, health human resource and facility management give little consideration to quality and performance as policies on quality of health care are fragmented, and quality standards and indicators have not been finalized and implemented widely. The overall governance structure for quality management at the central level, and the respective roles of subnational levels are still not clearly defined and remain patchy.

In this context, the TA[12] supports efforts to strengthen local governance for improving the quality of health care at the subnational level by (i) assisting in the improved implementation of quality of health care standards, (ii) increasing the availability of information on health care quality, and (iii) building local capacity for health care quality. The subproject works with the Ministry of Health, subnational health agencies, and health care facilities.

The subproject has helped to produce draft policy papers, including terms of reference (TORs) for quality committees, governance mechanisms for health care quality, a "5 Goods 1 Satisfaction" Quality Standard Framework, the "Dok Champa" Health Facility Accreditation Framework, a patient feedback mechanism, and various training materials targeting health officials and other stakeholders in the sector. The subproject organized a national conference to disseminate and discuss the draft knowledge products; it plans to conduct a series of regional training-of-trainers in 2021.

> **Launch meeting of the Quality Healthcare Committee.**
Participants during the organized national conference to disseminate and discuss the draft knowledge products of the subproject.

---

12   ADB. Regional: Strengthening Institutions for Localizing Agenda 2030 for Sustainable Development.

# 2 Regional Cooperation

## Regional: Assessing Economic Corridor Development Potential among Kazakhstan, Uzbekistan, and Tajikistan

**Sector:** Industry and Trade
**Amount:** $0.8 million

Central Asia is undergoing positive regional dynamics with the opening of Uzbekistan. Under the new circumstances, Central Asian countries—particularly Uzbekistan and neighboring Kazakhstan and Tajikistan—are keen to harness the potential of regional cooperation and integration (RCI) to promote growth, create jobs, and improve the quality of life of their citizens. Trade has been identified in these countries as an enabling driver in diversifying economies from a narrow base (overreliance on natural resources) into a more broad-based and sustainable growth model, for enhanced export competitiveness. Further, the growing trend of regional and global production networks, value chains, and new technologies, coupled with improved information and communication technology, create necessary conditions for Central Asia and CAREC member countries to increase participation in regional and global trade. Economic corridor development (ECD) provides an effective tool to promote trade integration among the three countries and realize economic benefits.

Challenges in developing the trilateral economic corridor include: weak performance of border crossing points, including substandard physical facilities and uncoordinated procedures, which weaken cross-border trade flows. Unharmonized trade policies and regulations add additional costs for non-Eurasian Economic Union (EAEU) firms in complying with EAEU requirements. Private sector participation in cross-border activities remains limited due to information asymmetry, weak incentives and insufficient conditions for investment, poor access to financing, and lack of effective dialogue with public sector stakeholders. These constraints must be eased to improve the environment for cross-border investment along the envisaged economic corridor. The ECD concept is not yet widely known to the CAREC countries. Thus, wider diffusion to the various communities and societies will help their understanding of the connections between ECD and growth, particularly the core concepts and key conditions for economic planning and development under a regional context.

The TA[13] supports scoping and prefeasibility studies to explore the ECD potentials of Shymkent–Tashkent–Khujand cities and surrounding Turkestan–Tashkent–Sughdoblasts. The TA will identify major constraints, gaps, and weak links—in terms of physical infrastructure connectivity and policy environment, including investment needed—in fully exploiting economic complementarities through an envisaged ECD. The TA will also support workshops and seminars that promote ECD-related knowledge sharing and awareness raising to enhance understanding and knowledge of ECD in the CAREC region. The benefits of the TA will be deepened economic cooperation and integration among the three countries through the trilateral economic corridor development, which will improve trade, create job opportunities (including for women by participating in cross-border activities such

---

13   ADB. Regional: Assessing Economic Corridor Development Potential Among Kazakhstan, Uzbekistan, and Tajikistan.

as tourism and trade), and promote entrepreneurship and private sector investment among the three countries. Key activities include an inception workshop in each of the three countries and multistakeholder consultation, and field work in May–August 2019, which identified priority sectors and areas for the trilateral economic corridor development. A first regional workshop in December 2019 discussed the vision and actions needed for the economic corridor development.

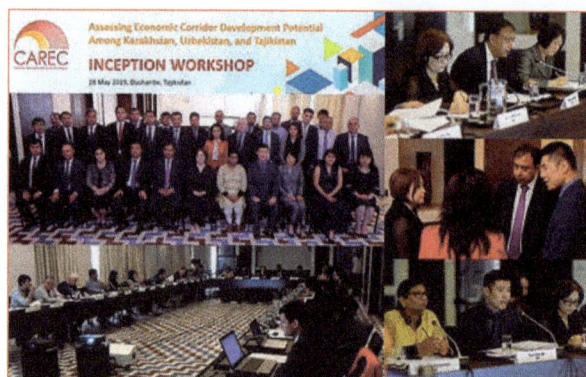

> **Technical assistance inception workshop in Kazakhstan and Tajikistan.** In the workshop, participants discussed regional economic corridor development potentials and challenges among Shymkent (Kazakhstan), Tashkent (Uzbekistan), and Khujand (Tajikistan) cities and their surrounding regions.

> **Technical assistance inception workshop in Uzbekistan.** In the workshop, participants discussed regional economic corridor development potentials and challenges among Shymkent (Kazakhstan), Tashkent (Uzbekistan), and Khujand (Tajikistan) cities and their surrounding regions.

> **Site visits in Kazakhstan, Tajikistan, and Uzbekistan.** Participants visited several production sites in Kazakhstan, Tajikistan, and Uzbekistan, which aim to help identify priority sectors and areas for the trilateral economic corridor development.

## Regional: Strengthening Asia's Financial Safety Nets and Resolution Mechanisms

**Sector:** Public Sector Management

**Amount:** $125,000

Increases in levels in nonperforming loans (NPLs) in some economies in the region alarm policy makers and market players alike, as these may lead to financial vulnerabilities, contagion, and systemic risks. Thus, NPL management and resolution remain the focus of discussions on safeguarding financial stability.

Identifying and developing strategies for national NPL resolution mechanisms and the development of NPL or distressed asset markets in emerging Asia would strengthen financial stability and resilience in Asia. Developing markets for distressed assets is a challenge that requires policy efforts to build necessary financial market infrastructure, address legal and institutional weaknesses, and review and revise supervisory guidelines and regulatory standards to facilitate NPL write-offs. Each economy faces different conditions that must be considered in developing a distressed asset market—including legal, regulatory, and institutional frameworks; financial market and infrastructure development; and fiscal situation. Hence, each development experience offers valuable lessons applicable to the region.

The TA[14] aims to address the issue of NPLs in the Asia and Pacific region by supporting the development of a national strategy and a market for NPLs or distressed assets through research and capacity building. This will be coupled with knowledge sharing through Annual Summit Meetings and Conferences of the International Public Asset Management Company Forum (IPAF), as well as training workshops to build the capacity of public asset management companies, deposit insurance institutions, and other invited regional participants to manage distressed assets.

Since the start of TA implementation, the following main activities have been implemented:

1. **4th IPAF Summit and Conference**, 15–16 November 2018, Ha Noi, Viet Nam. ERCD and Viet Nam Debt and Asset Trading Corporation co-organized the summit and conference that focused on Asia's latest economic and financial trends, financial safety nets, and strategies of NPL market development. The events were also joined by the Republic of Korea Financial Services Commission, the World Bank, the European Central Bank, the Central Bank of Bangladesh, and the Central Bank of Mongolia.

2. **6th Training Seminar: Effective Legal and Operational Frameworks for NPL Resolution**, 27–28 May 2019, Ha Noi, Viet Nam. ERCD, together with Viet Nam Debt and Asset Trading Corporation and Viet Nam Asset Management Corporation, organized this training seminar which focused on the systemic role of NPLs through case studies and comparative analyses on operational and legal challenges for NPL resolution and NPL market development in Asia and Europe. The seminar was attended by more than 70 participants, including the academia, legal experts, financial institutions from the People's Republic of China, the Republic of Korea, Kazakhstan, the European Central Bank, the Bank of Thailand; and 10 government officials from the Ministry of Finance, the State Bank of Vietnam, and the National Financial Supervisory Commission.

3. **5th IPAF Summit and Conference**, 25–26 September 2019, Seoul, Republic of Korea. These events focused on harnessing IPAF for promoting Asian NPL markets. The role of IPAF was highlighted as the forum to serve as a useful platform for identifying strategies to develop national and regional NPL markets. The conference stressed the need for Asia to swiftly and effectively manage and respond to a buildup of financial instability; strengthen development of NPL markets under financial market development plans; and work collectively in risk identification, mitigation, and response.

---

14  ADB. Regional: Strengthening Asia's Financial Safety Nets and Resolution Mechanisms.

4.      Publication of **Strengthening Asia's Financial Safety Net**[15] in December 2019. This report provides a useful synthesis of the elements comprising Asia's financial safety net, examines the evolution and the tool kits of regional financing arrangements, and assesses the complementary role of ADB in providing crisis response mechanisms through its policy-based lending facilities.

5.      The following reports are being finalized for publication soon: (i) Strategies for Developing Asia's NPL Markets and Resolution Mechanisms; and (ii) Country Case Studies on Resolving Problem Loans in Europe: Crises, Policies, and Institutions. These will also be part of the edited volume on Non-Performing Loans in Asia and Europe: Causes, Impacts, and Resolution Strategies, expected to be published by the end of 2020.

> **6th International Public Asset Management Company Forum Training Seminar.** Over 70 officials from public asset management corporations, deposit insurance corporations, private financial institutions, and government offices participated in the seminar on 27–28 May 2019 in Ha Noi.

> **4th International Public Asset Management Company Forum International Conference.** Representatives from IPAF members, other asset management companies, banks, Viet Nam government agencies, development partners, the academia, private sector, and media attended the conference with the theme "A Road to Strengthening Asia's Financial Safety Nets and Resolution Mechanisms" on 15 November 2018 in Ha Noi.

> **5th International Public Asset Management Company Forum International Conference.** Representatives from IPAF members, other asset management companies, banks, Republic of Korea government agencies, the academia, private sector, and media attended the conference with the theme "Harnessing IPAF for Promoting Asian NPL Markets" on 26 September 2019 in Seoul.

---

15   ADB. 2019. *Strengthening Asia's Financial Safety Net.* Manila. https://www.adb.org/publications/strengthening-asia-financial-safety-net.

# 3 Knowledge Sharing

## Regional: Enhancing Regional Knowledge Sharing Partnerships
**Sector:** Public Sector Management
**Amount:** $0.75 million

The TA[16] approved in June 2018 supports the activities of the ADB–PRC Regional Knowledge Sharing Initiative (RKSI).[17] RKSI is a knowledge sharing platform that aims to share development lessons among ADB's developing member countries (DMCs), in particular, the experience of the PRC in supporting rapid economic growth over the past 40 years. Since its inception in 2012, the PRC Fund has funded RKSI's activities focusing on five themes, two of which are the key pillars of the PRC Fund, while the others are economic transformation, climate change and environmental management, and urban development.

In 2019, RKSI successfully, among others: (i) designed, funded, and implemented 36 knowledge sharing events (conferences, workshops, and seminars) with 14 external partners benefiting over 2,800 participants; and (ii) co-organized and contributed to the first (and now the ongoing second) global solicitation of best poverty reduction case studies. Of the 36 events, 8 focused primarily on poverty reduction and regional cooperation involving over 900 participants. With the International Poverty Reduction Center in China and other partners, RKSI organized five poverty reduction events, three of which were regular RKSI supported events: the *8th ASEAN+3 Village Leaders Exchange Programme*, *13th ASEAN–China Forum on Social Development and Poverty Reduction*, and *China Poverty Reduction International Forum*.

The Village Leaders Exchange Program focused on building capacity of village leaders, while the ASEAN–China Forum targeted knowledge sharing at the official level. Both aimed to share good practices and innovative ideas on poverty reduction between the PRC and Association of Southeast Asian Nations (ASEAN), and discuss ways to enhance poverty reduction partnerships. A unique benefit of the Village Leaders Exchange Program was the homestay at a village transformed out of poverty for participants to witness firsthand the new daily life of villagers. Meanwhile, the China Poverty Reduction International Forum is the PRC's premier knowledge sharing event on poverty reduction with the rest of the world. Last year's highlight was the announcement of 110 best poverty reduction practices from around the world. These cases, covering a diverse range of successful poverty reduction initiatives, would benefit policy makers and researchers who are interested to learn and apply them in their respective countries. RKSI's contributed two cases from the PRC and coordinated the submission of seven cases from ADB, which were all awarded as best practices. These cases also came out as an ADB publication titled *Effective Approaches to Poverty Reduction: Selected Cases from the Asian Development Bank*.[18]

---

16  ADB. Regional: Enhancing Regional Knowledge Sharing Partnerships.
17  ADB–PRC Regional Knowledge Sharing Initiative (RKSI). http://rksi.org/.
18  ADB. 2019. *Effective Approaches to Poverty Reduction: Selected Cases from the Asian Development Bank*. Manila. https://www.adb.org/publications/approaches-poverty-reduction-cases-adb.

On regional cooperation, RKSI continued to support the Central Asia Regional Economic Cooperation (CAREC) Institute in its flagship *CAREC Think Tank Development Forum*, which promotes the networking and exchange of views and knowledge on evolving regional and global policy challenges among countries in Central and West Asia. Last year's forum on *Trading for Shared Prosperity* identified and discussed main challenges to trade within the region, among which were economic implications of the burgeoning trade conflicts among major global trading partners.

Separately, RKSI also supported *Inter-Subregional Knowledge-Sharing Forum: Trade Facilitation and Customs Modernization for the CAREC and South Asia Subregional Economic Cooperation (SASEC) Programs.* Customs representatives from the two regions who attended benefited from the sharing of knowledge, experience, and best practices on trade facilitation reforms and modernization efforts on overland trade facing their customs administrations. This exchange was expected to be a step toward improving trade flows, resource allocations, and regional cooperation between the two regions.

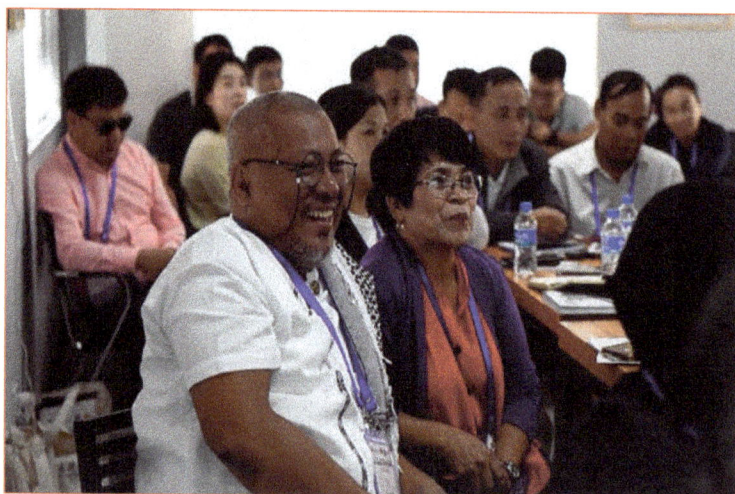

> **8th ASEAN+3 Village Leaders Exchange Programme,** Participants attended program held in Xishuangbanna, Yunnan, the PRC on 5–11 May 2019, where they shared good practices and innovative ideas on poverty reduction and discussed ways to enhance poverty reduction partnerships.

> **China Poverty Reduction International Forum.** The event in Beijing, the People's Republic of China on 17 October 2019 highlighted the launch of the Second Global Solicitation on Best Practice in Poverty Reduction, where 110 best poverty reduction practices that cover a diverse range of successful poverty reduction initiatives were identified.

> **4th CAREC Think Tanks Development Forum.** A representative from China Logistics Association introduced the transportation and logistics standards along the Silk Road in Xian, the People's Republic of China on 27–28 August 2019.

# Regional: Developing an Accountability Mechanism Framework for Financial Intermediaries

**Sector:** Finance
**Amount:** $225,000

The activities in this TA[19] addressed the need to increase the social accountability of financial intermediaries (FIs) that are on-lending funds from international financial institutions. Through the TA, establishing an independent and accessible complaint redress mechanism at the regional, national, and institutional levels was elevated as a business imperative and not just a corporate social responsibility.

Through this TA, a regional workshop was held in Shanghai, PRC in May 2019 where the draft regional Accountability Mechanism Framework (AMF) developed by the TA international consultant was presented. The participants from 16 DMCs exchanged views and gave comments to improve the draft. The workshop attracted keen interest from the PRC's government agencies to develop their own national AMF, which led to a change in TA scope to support this initiative. The TA national consultant assisted in the preparation of the national AMF for PRC and organized a focused consultative workshop in Beijing in July 2019 to enrich this national AMF.

In parallel, the ADB Office of the Compliance Review Panel (OCRP) coordinated with the participants from Indonesia and India to gauge their interest in pursuing the development of their country- or institution-specific AMFs and offered support should they decide to work on those further. While these participants were keen to improve their social and environmental compliance and monitoring framework and their complaint handling system, they believed that, at that time, they could not pursue a more active involvement in shaping an AMF (similar to the AMF that was presented in the Shanghai workshop) for their institutions or for their country since they were from the private sector.

---

[19] ADB. Regional: Central Asia Regional Economic Cooperation: Supporting Capacity Development Needs of CAREC 2020.

A wrap-up workshop was held in Manila on October 2019 to present the regional AMF: *Safeguard Compliance and Accountability Framework for Investments Supported by Financial Intermediaries*,[20] and the PRC national AMF: *Policy Framework for Environmental and Social Safeguard Compliance and the Grievance Redress Mechanism of Overseas Investment and Financing Projects by Chinese Financial Institutions*.[21] The workshop also highlighted current initiatives by India and Indonesia at improving their systems toward adopting an AMF in the future. The wrap-up workshop, which included selected ADB staff as participants, identified the critical need for government support in establishing national and institutional AMFs to ensure greater accountability to persons adversely affected by projects whose funds are on-lent by FIs. For this, partnerships with ADB and key FIs are needed, particularly in supporting policy dialogues with relevant government agencies and financial support for capacity building of these agencies.

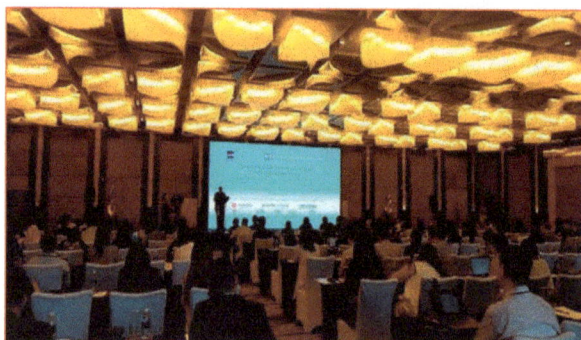

**The ADB Office of the Compliance Review Panel regional workshop.** Participants from state-owned banks and other financial intermediaries, and representatives from multilateral development banks, the Government of the People's Republic of China, research institutes, nongovernment organizations or civil society organizations, and other developing member countries during the workshop.

**Seminar on Environmental and Social Safeguard Compliance and Accountability Mechanism Framework for Financial Intermediaries.** Participants discussed the draft National Framework on the Accountability Mechanism for the People's Republic of China's financial intermediaries developed by the ADB Office of the Compliance Review Panel.

**Workshop on developing an accountability mechanism framework for financial intermediaries.** The 1-day workshop presented and discussed the draft regional and People's Republic of China's national accountability mechanism frameworks, along with representatives from the PRC, India, and Indonesia with the view of enhancing the technical assistance outputs.

---

[20] ADB. 2019. *Safeguard Compliance and Accountability Framework for Investments Supported by Financial Intermediaries.* https://www.adb.org/projects/documents/reg-53140-001-tacr-0.

[21] ADB. 2019. *Policy Framework for Environmental and Social Safeguard Compliance and the Grievance Redress Mechanism of Overseas Investment and Financing Projects by Chinese Financial Institutions.* https://www.adb.org/projects/documents/reg-53140-001-tacr.

# Regional: Central Asia Regional Economic Cooperation: Supporting Capacity Development Needs of CAREC 2020

**Sector:** Industry and Trade
**Amount:** $0.9 million

The TA[22] supports the effective and efficient implementation of priority CAREC projects with regional dimension and mutual benefits for CAREC countries. The PRC Fund funding was used to push for improvement of the capacity of CAREC member countries to plan, manage, and implement projects that contribute to the goals and objectives of CAREC 2020. In close collaboration with the CAREC Institute (CI), the PRC Fund supported capacity-building and knowledge sharing activities to achieve the project outcome of improving the capacity of CAREC countries to plan, manage, and implement projects and activities that contribute to the goals of CAREC 2020. In 2019, the PRC Fund supported nine events of the CI. Among these, a major event, *4th CAREC Think Tanks Development Forum* (CTTDF),[23] was organized with the topic of "Trading for Shared Prosperity" on 28–29 August 2019 in Xian, Shaanxi province, PRC. About 130 participants representing governments, think tanks, research institutions, and development partners from 20 countries attended the event.

Through the project, CAREC 2020 called on the CI to strengthen capacities of various stakeholders to support the achievement of CAREC's strategic goals. The conduct of high-level forums, seminars, and dialogues involving internationally renowned experts on CAREC priority and cross-sector concerns is part of the TA's deliverables and support for the 4th CTTDF is in line with the PRC Fund's third pillar of knowledge sharing. In addition, the forum was widely disseminated and broadcasted through various communication channels. The knowledge generated from the said events provided solutions for CAREC member countries on respective cross-sector concerns.

The 4th CTTDF became a venue for strong collaboration for think tanks, the academia, and governments from the CAREC region to exchange views and knowledge on evolving regional and global policy challenges. The 4th CTTDF discussed regional integration, ongoing trade disputes, standardizing logistics along the Silk Road, technological interventions, e-commerce and its impacts on the regional economy, and preliminary findings of the CAREC Think Tanks Network (CTTN) research grants program. Trade expansion from increased market access and greater diversification under the CAREC Integrated Trade Agenda (CITA) 2030 was also discussed. This forum benefited CAREC member countries on trade prosperity.

The CTTDF is organized annually by CI under the auspices of the CAREC Think Tanks Network (CTTN). The CTTN promotes regional economic cooperation by enhancing systemic regional knowledge sharing and integration; fostering policy research and knowledge solutions to support governments; enabling better policy advice; reducing gaps between research and policy; and enhancing collective intelligence to consolidate development resources for effective cooperation, better services, and improved performance. The CTTDF has become an attractive destination for think tanks, the academia, and governments from the CAREC region and beyond to exchange views and knowledge on evolving regional and global policy challenges. ADB plans to support the 5th CTTDF to be organized in 2021.

---

22 ADB. Regional: Central Asia Regional Economic Cooperation: Supporting Capacity Development Needs of CAREC 2020.
23 CAREC Institute. https://www.carecinstitute.com/news/the-4th-carec-think-tanks-forum-concludes.

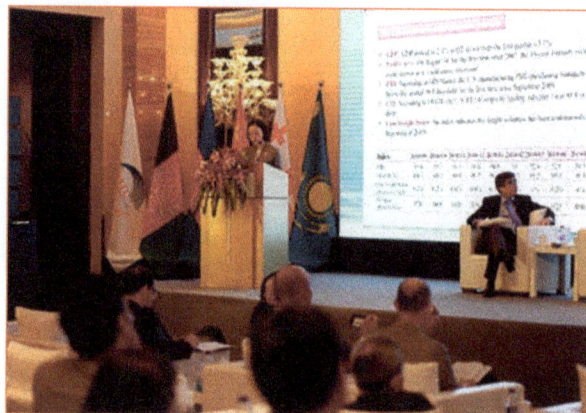

> **4th CAREC Think Tanks Development Forum in Xian, Shaanxi province, People's Republic of China.**

The 4th CTTDF convened over 130 participants from over 20 countries coming from think tanks, the academia, the private sector, and governments to deliberate on trade expansion from increased market access, greater diversification, and stronger institutions for trade under the CAREC Integrated Trade Agenda 2030.

A representative from the International Economics and Finance Institute at the Ministry of Finance of the PRC spoke about five ongoing global trade conflicts which have an impact on the Asian economy: United States (US)–PRC, US–Japan, US–European Union, US–Mexico, and Japan–Republic of Korea.

# Transaction Technical Assistance Projects Supported by PRC Fund

ADB provides technical assistance (TA) for the preparation, financing, and execution of development projects and programs, including the formulation of specific project proposals. It may also provide TA to assist members in the coordination of their development policies and plans. TA facilitates the channeling of ADB's financial assistance to the developing member countries (DMCs). It also improves the capacity of DMCs to absorb external assistance and further their economic development.

One type of TA, transaction technical assistance (TRTA) directly benefits an ongoing project being supported by ADB or a project being processed for ADB financing. TRTA covers: (i) project preparation, (ii) project implementation capacity support, (iii) policy advice toward policy-based operations, or (iii) development of a public–private partnership under transaction advisory services.

In 2019, the PRC Fund prioritized support for TRTA, particularly project preparation to better meet the requirements of ADB's Strategy 2030 and establish closer links with ADB's main operations. In fact, the PRC Ministry of Finance (MOF) has approved three TRTA projects totaling $4.1 million to support sectors such as water and other urban infrastructure and services, and energy (Boxes 1–3).

**Box 1: Regional: Preparing Sustainable Energy Projects in Central Asia**

**Sector:** Energy
**Amount:** $1.6 million

The regional transaction technical assistance (TRTA) facility will provide project preparation support to a series of ensuing projects in Central Asia, comprising: (i) Power Distribution Enhancement, Renewable Energy and Energy Efficiency Projects in the Kyrgyz Republic; and (ii) Power Sector Development Program in the Republic of Tajikistan. In addition, the TRTA facility will provide high-level screening, due diligence, and formulation of the components for the Sector Development Project in Kazakhstan.

The electricity sector of Central Asia, developed during the time of the former Soviet Union, was primarily designed to optimize the use of water resources, with electricity being a secondary product. Power plants and transmission lines were built without consideration of the administrative boundaries, which later became national borders. After the collapse of the Soviet Union in 1991, the energy ministers of the Central Asian states faced a new challenge of autonomously operating national power grids that were not designed to operate as such. In addition to technical complexities, the energy sector in these countries followed different development paths.

The proposed ADB intervention intends to address various sector issues, including refurbishment of the power generators, construction of new transmission assets, energy efficiency, renewable energy generation, and introduction of modern technologies.

The People's Republic of China Poverty Reduction and Regional Cooperation Fund (PRC Fund) supports key preparatory activities such as procurement capacity assessment; technical, financial, economic, and safeguards due diligence; financial management assessment; risk assessment; as well as knowledge sharing activities such as training programs, workshops, and seminars.

Source: ADB. Regional: Preparing Sustainable Energy Projects in Central Asia.

## Box 2: Uzbekistan: Preparing Urban Development and Improvement Projects

**Sector:** Water and Other Urban Infrastructure and Services
**Amount: $1.0 million**

ADB will apply a comprehensive and programmatic approach to develop more integrated urban development solutions. The transaction technical assistance (TRTA) facility will provide project preparation support to a series of ensuing projects, comprising: (i) Tashkent Province Sewerage Improvement Project ($160 million), (ii) Uzbekistan Water Supply and Sanitation Development Program ($200 million), (iii) Uzbekistan Integrated Urban Development Project ($200 million), and (iv) Uzbekistan Solid Waste Management Development Project ($150 million). The TRTA facility will support improvement of water supply and sanitation and other public services through technical, policy, and capacity development in both urban and rural areas. Uzbekistan now has stronger country systems and capacity and using the principle-based sector program approach, will give the country a greater sense of ownership. An integrated approach will be applied to the development of economic growth clusters with stronger urban rural linkages. Support in these areas, including tourism development, will cover urban planning and management, urban rural linkages and provision of public services, cultural heritage protection, information and communication technology, public–private partnership arrangements, and small and medium-sized enterprises and women business enterprise development.

The People's Republic of China Poverty Reduction and Regional Cooperation Fund (PRC Fund) supports project activities for capacity building and technical outputs, including: (i) development of integrated urban master plans for selected cities and towns through participatory and inclusive processes and geographic information system spatial mapping; (ii) preparation of an urbanization policy, road map, and framework for selected towns; (iii) supporting study visits and establishing peer-to-peer learning (twinning) programs for high-level policy makers and technical staff to relevant countries; and (iv) a workshop to share knowledge on good practices in strategic and planned urban growth, including examples from the PRC and other countries.

Source: ADB. Uzbekistan: Preparing Urban Development and Improvement Projects.

## Box 3: Pakistan: Preparing Urban Development Projects

**Sector:** Water and Other Urban Infrastructure and Services
**Amount: $1.5 million**

The transaction technical assistance (TRTA) facility will support urban sector analyses, project preparation and capacity development, and project due diligence during 2019–2021 in a series of urban development investment projects. These projects will comprise the subsectors of: (i) urban transport; (ii) urban water, sanitation, and flood control; (iii) solid waste management; (iv) low-income housing; (v) cultural heritage restoration; (vi) tourism development; and (vii) information and communication technology. To develop these projects, preparatory work in the form of feasibility studies, environmental and social safeguards work, financial management assessments, and economic analyses will be required. The TA facility is included in the current Country Operations Business Plan (COBP), 2019–2021 for Pakistan.

The People's Republic of China Poverty Reduction and Regional Cooperation Fund (PRC Fund) supports project preparatory work and capacity building activities covering the following components: (i) project feasibility studies, (ii) deepening of due diligence and safeguards work for the investment projects, and (iii) additional project preparatory studies and capacity development for the investment project.

Source: ADB. Pakistan: Preparing Urban Development Projects.

# Chapter 3

# Overview of Fund Operations, 2005–2019

## Cumulative Approvals

A total of 112 applications amounting to $56.39 million were approved between March 2005 and December 2019.[24] These included seven approvals of supplementary funding and two applications combined with prior approvals. The 112 approved applications represented 103 projects, of which 100 are technical assistance totaling $53.84 million and 3 are grant projects totaling $2.55 million. Of the 103 approved projects, 66 (64%) have financially closed and 35 (34%) remain active; in the case of 2 other projects, the period for ADB approval, under Fund Implementation Guidelines, has elapsed and the funding allocation has been returned to the Fund pool. Appendix 2 provides a detailed list of all approved project applications from 2005 to 2019.

## Cumulative Project Performance

As of 31 December 2019, 58 of the 66 completed projects had technical assistance completion report (TCR) ratings.[25] Of the 58 projects supported by the Fund, 51 were rated *highly successful* (16%) or *successful* (72%), with a combined success rate of 88%. The combined success rate of 88% matches the 86% 3-year success rate reported in the latest Development Effectiveness Report.[26]

## Cumulative Portfolio Distribution

**Geographic distribution.** Regional[27] projects received the largest share (82%). Of this, 23% went to CAREC[28] and 21% to the GMS,[29] indicating the priority assigned to these regions in line with fund objectives. The rest (37%) went to other regional projects, including ASEAN+3 projects and projects

---

24  Of the 115 approved applications, 112 totaling $56.39 million were approved between 2005 and 2019 by the PRC Ministry of Finance (MOF) and 3 others worth $1.75 million were approved in the first 3 months of 2020.

25  The TCR ratings for the main project and the supplementary project were counted as one.

26  ADB. 2020. *Development Effectiveness Review 2019*. Manila.

27  Regional projects are projects that fall exclusively under CAREC or the GMS, or under (i) a mix of various regions and subregional programs (e.g., CAREC and APEC, the GMS and ASEAN+3) and (ii) a mix of various countries in only one region (e.g., Central Asia, Southeast Asia, East Asia).

28  The CAREC Program is a partnership of 11 countries (Afghanistan, Azerbaijan, Georgia, Kazakhstan, Kyrgyz Republic, Mongolia, Pakistan, the People's Republic of China, Tajikistan, Turkmenistan, and Uzbekistan), supported by six multilateral institutions, and working together to promote development through cooperation, leading to accelerated growth and poverty reduction.

29  The Greater Mekong Subregion consists of Cambodia, the Lao People's Democratic Republic (Lao PDR), Myanmar, the People's Republic of China (PRC, specifically Yunnan Province and Guangxi Zhuang Autonomous Region), Thailand, and Viet Nam.

in Asia-Pacific Economic Cooperation (APEC)[30] member economies. Country-specific projects accounted for 18% of fund support, distributed among countries in Central Asia (9%), South Asia (4%), Southeast Asia (2%), East Asia (2%), and the Pacific (1%) (Figure 6).

**Sector distribution.** Public sector management (28%), energy (16%), industry and trade (16%), and water and other urban infrastructure and services (11%) made up more than half of Fund approvals. The rest was distributed among agriculture, natural resources, and rural development (8%); multisector (7%); and the finance, transport, education, health, and information and communication technology sectors (14%) (Figure 7).

**ADB department distribution.** The regional departments received 73% of the total Fund support. This went mainly to CWRD (27%) and SERD (25%), reflecting the prominence of assistance to the CAREC and the GMS regions. The rest of the Fund was distributed among EARD (16%), SARD (4%), and Pacific Department (PARD) (1%). Funding for knowledge and capacity development projects (20%) was distributed between SDCC (12%) and the Economic Research and Regional Cooperation Department (ERCD) (8%). The remaining 6% financed the activities of various departments and offices, including results-based monitoring and evaluation by the Independent Evaluation Department (IED) (3%). The Office of Public–Private Partnership (OPPP), Procurement, Portfolio and Financial Management Department (PPFD), and the Office of the Compliance Review Panel (OCRP) each received 1% of the Fund (Figure 8).

**Figure 6:** **Geographic Distribution, 2015–2019**
(% share of total amount)

Regional **82%**
Country-specific **18%**

CAREC = Central Asia Regional Economic Cooperation,
GMS = Greater Mekong Subregion.
Notes:
1. "Other" refers to projects that involve countries in only one region or from two or more regions.
2. Percentages may not total 100% because of rounding.
Source: ADB database.

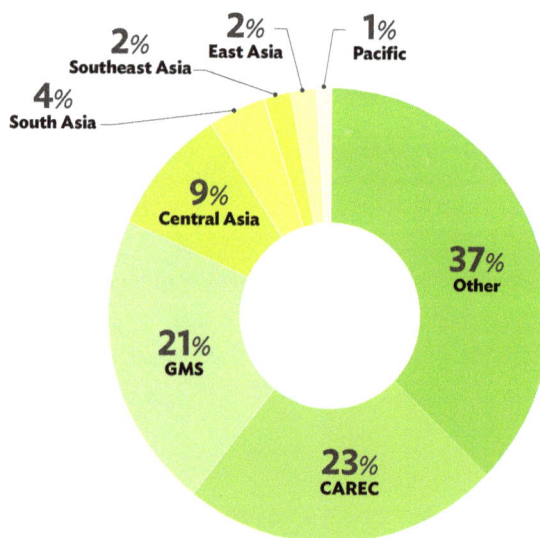

---

[30] APEC comprises 21 member economies: Australia; Brunei Darussalam; Canada; Chile; Hong Kong, China; Indonesia; Japan; Malaysia; Mexico; New Zealand; Papua New Guinea; the People's Republic of China; Peru; the Philippines; the Republic of Korea; the Russian Federation; Singapore; Taipei,China; Thailand; the United States; and Viet Nam.

**Figure 7: Sector Distribution, 2005–2019**
(% share of total amount)

Source: ADB database.

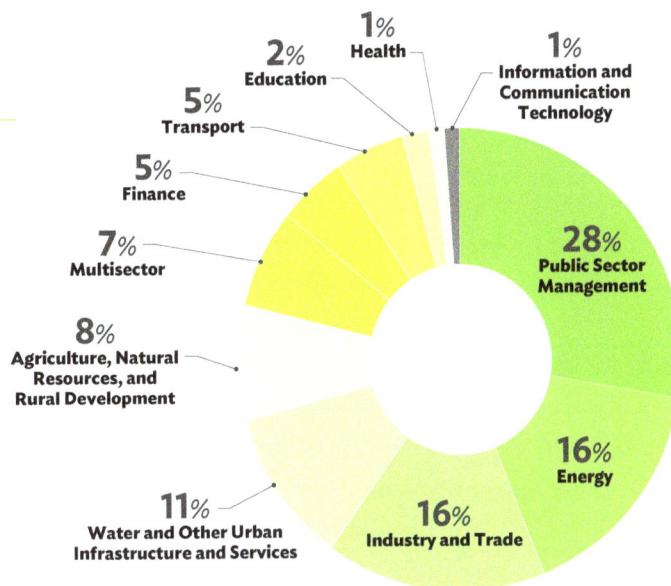

- 1% Health
- 2% Education
- 5% Transport
- 5% Finance
- 7% Multisector
- 8% Agriculture, Natural Resources, and Rural Development
- 11% Water and Other Urban Infrastructure and Services
- 1% Information and Communication Technology
- 28% Public Sector Management
- 16% Energy
- 16% Industry and Trade

**Figure 8: ADB Department Distribution, 2019**
(% share of total amount)

ADB = Asian Development Bank, CWRD = Central and West Asia Department, EARD = East Asia Department, ERCD = Economic Research and Regional Cooperation Department, IED = Independent Evaluation Department, OCRP = Office of the Compliance Review Panel, OPPP = Office of Public–Private Partnership, PARD = Pacific Department, PPFD = Procurement, Portfolio and Financial Management Department, SARD = South Asia Department, SDCC = Sustainable Development and Climate Change Department, SERD = Southeast Asia Department.
Source: ADB database.

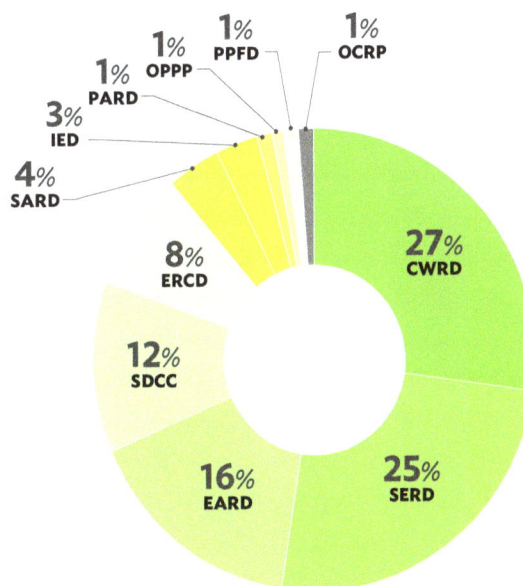

- 1% OPPP
- 1% PPFD
- 1% OCRP
- 1% PARD
- 3% IED
- 4% SARD
- 8% ERCD
- 12% SDCC
- 16% EARD
- 27% CWRD
- 25% SERD

# Chapter 4

# Partnering: The Way Forward

In 2019, the Fund approved 10 projects supporting ADB's efforts in fighting poverty and promoting regional cooperation and integration through enhanced linkage with the Belt and Road Initiative (BRI), the CAREC Program, and the GMS in Asia and the Pacific.

With its uncommitted balance of $36.27 million as of 31 December 2019 for future allocations,[31] the Fund will continue to strengthen its support for ADB's seven operational priorities under Strategy 2030 and encourage synergies across various regional cooperation initiatives, particularly BRI, CAREC, and the GMS, and further improve its services to ADB and its DMC clients for their economic and social development.

---

[31] Allocations refer to new projects and administrative cost; available balance includes contribution receivables coming in 2019 and 2020 (the 2019 installment was delivered in April 2019), and is net of allocations approved by the PRC MOF and awaiting ADB approval.

# Appendix 1

# Brief Summaries of PRC Fund Projects Approved in 2019

## Energy Sector

| | Impact | Outcome | Outputs |
|---|---|---|---|
| **Grant 0675-BAN: Dhaka and Western Zone Transmission Grid Expansion Project[a]** Amount: $750,000 | National target of electricity for all achieved by 2021 (Perspective Plan of Bangladesh, 2010–2021: Making Vision 2021 a Reality). | Reliability and efficiency of electricity supply in Greater Dhaka and western zone of Bangladesh improved. | 1. Transmission system in Greater Dhaka expanded. 2. Transmission system in western zone expanded. 3. Institutional capacity of Power Grid Company of Bangladesh Limited strengthened. |
| **TA 9938-MON: Methane Gas Supply Chain Development Master Plan[b]** Amount: $500,000 | 1. Air quality improved (National Program on Reduction of Air and Environmental Pollution). 2. Reliable and cleaner energy supply secured (Implementation Plan for the Government Action Plan, 2016–2020). | Readiness for investments in methane gas supply infrastructure increased. | 1. Methane gas supply chain development strategy paper prepared. 2. Prefeasibility study report on prioritized methane gas infrastructure projects prepared. 3. Capacity in methane gas supply infrastructure enhanced. |
| **TA 9792-REG: Preparing Sustainable Energy Projects in Central Asia[c]** Amount: $1,600,000 | The regional transaction TA facility will provide project preparation support to a series of ensuing projects in Central Asia, comprising: (i) Power Distribution Enhancement, Renewable Energy and Energy Efficiency Projects in the Kyrgyz Republic; and (ii) Power Sector Development Program in the Republic of Tajikistan. In addition, the TA facility will provide high-level screening, due diligence, and formulation of the components for the Sector Development Project in Kazakhstan. All ensuing projects are in the energy sector and require a similar set of safeguards, financial management, or economic assessments. | | 1. Power Distribution Enhancement, Renewable Energy and Energy Efficiency Projects in the Kyrgyz Republic prepared. 2. Power Sector Development Program in the Republic of Tajikistan prepared. 3. High-level screening and preliminary assessment of potential energy projects for Energy Sector Development Program or a new project in Kazakhstan prepared. |

## Water and Other Urban Infrastructure and Services Sector

| | Impact | Outcome | Outputs |
|---|---|---|---|
| **TA 9715-UZB: Preparing Urban Development and Improvement Projects (Supplementary)[d] Amount: $1,000,000** | The transaction TA facility will help to prepare interrelated projects and TA. It will ensure a consistent approach to urban development, address cross-sector themes, develop local capacity for improved project implementation, enhance project readiness, and strengthen overall coordination and cooperation for the country's sustainable urban development. The design of the transaction TA facility follows ADB's sector and thematic operational plans, namely the Water Operational Plan 2011–2020, Urban Operational Plan 2012–2020, and the Environmental Operational Directions 2013–2020 and will contribute to key operation priorities such as livable cities, governance and institutional capacity improvement, and environmental sustainability enhancement under Strategy 2030. | Investment and TA projects suitable for ADB financing prepared. | 1. Technical feasibility assessments conducted and technical specifications prepared. 2. Safeguard due diligence of the ensuing projects and documentation completed. 3. Investment plans and procurement packages prepared. 4. Sustainable business model and institutional capacity developed. |
| **TA 9839-PAK: Preparing Urban Development Projects[e] Amount: $1,500,000** | The COBP 2019–2021 for Pakistan includes investments to promote at least three operational priorities of ADB Strategy 2030: (i) promote the creation of more livable cities using integrated solutions; (ii) incorporate climate resilience, integrated environmental management, and gender mainstreaming into city planning processes; and (iii) strengthen governance and institutional capacity for financial sustainability. The TA facility will support preparatory activities for ensuing projects and innovative aspects of ongoing projects in need of further preparatory activities. | Investment projects suitable for ADB financing prepared. | 1. Feasibility studies and investment plans prepared. 2. Due diligence for ensuing projects completed. 3. Project management and urban service delivery capacity strengthened. |

## Transport Sector

| | Impact | Outcome | Outputs |
|---|---|---|---|
| **TA 9918-REG: Connecting the Railways of the Greater Mekong Subregion, (Phase 2)[f] Amount: $500,000** | Greater railway connectivity in the GMS provided (Greater Mekong Subregion Economic Cooperation Program Strategic Framework, 2012–2022)[a] | GMRA functioning with adequate capacity and funding | 1. Organizational structure of the GMRA improved. 2. Operational readiness plan for the GMRA developed. 3. GMS railway network development strategy updated. 4. Updated the GMS transport demand model prepared. 5. Bankable railway projects identified in the GMS countries. |

## Agriculture, Natural Resources, and Rural Development Sector

| | Impact | Outcome | Outputs |
|---|---|---|---|
| **TA 9846-REG: Developing Partnerships for Knowledge Sharing on Natural Capital Investment in the Yangtze River Economic Belt[g] Amount: $225,000** | More DMCs benefited from the YREB knowledge sharing with the partnership initiative established by the TA (YREB Development Plan, 2016–2030)[a] | International partnership initiative for the YREB knowledge sharing established | 1. International partnership initiative for knowledge sharing on natural capital investment in the YREB developed. 2. Workshops to develop the partnership and consultation on the initiative organized. 3. Partnership initiative officially launched. |

## Public and Management Sector

| | Impact | Outcome | Outputs |
|---|---|---|---|
| **TA 9791-REG: Strengthening Fiscal Governance and Sustainability in Public–Private Partnerships (Supplementary)[h]** Amount: $500,000 | Fiscal sustainability of PPP investments in infrastructure projects promoted in DMCs (ADB Strategy 2030).[a] | Capacity to integrate fiscally sustainable PPPs improved in selected DMCs. | 1. Policy, legal, regulatory, and institutional frameworks for PPP development and management strengthened in DMCs. 2. PFM and fiscal risk management for legacy and new PPPs strengthened in DMCs. 3. Policy experience on creating fiscally sustainable PPPs disseminated to DMCs. |

## Industry and Trade Sector

| | Impact | Outcome | Outputs |
|---|---|---|---|
| **TA 9824-REG: Better Customs for Better Client Services in Central Asia Regional Economic Cooperation Countries[i]** Amount: $500,000 | 1. Trade and smooth flow of goods and people across the CAREC region increased (CAREC 2030).[a] 2. Trade from increased market access expanded (CAREC Integrated Trade Agenda [CITA] 2030).[b] | CAREC customs agencies and the Customs Cooperation Committee providing better services to their clients. | 1. Scoping studies with actionable recommendations in customs infrastructure, facilities, use of technology, and logistics support prepared. 2. Initiatives in modern customs technologies and best practice supported. 3. Customs capacity improved. |

## Finance Sector

| | Impact | Outcome | Outputs |
|---|---|---|---|
| **TA 9718-REG: Developing an Accountability Mechanism Framework for Financial Intermediaries[j]** Amount: $225,000 | Development effectiveness and accountability to project affected persons improved. | Safeguard compliance supervision and accountability to project affected persons improved by financial intermediaries (FIs). | Draft Accountability Mechanism Framework (AMF) for FIs developed. |

ADB = Asian Development Bank, BAN = Bangladesh, CAM = Cambodia, CAREC = Central Asia Regional Economic Cooperation, COBP = country operations business plan, DMC = developing member country, GMRA = Greater Mekong Railway Association, GMS = Greater Mekong Subregion, MON = Mongolia, MYA = Myanmar, NEP = Nepal, PAK = Pakistan, PFM = public financial management, PPP = public–private partnership, PRC Fund = People's Republic of China Poverty Reduction and Regional Cooperation Fund, REG = regional, TA = technical assistance, UZB = Uzbekistan, YREB = Yangtze River Economic Belt.

[a] ADB. 2019. *Report and Recommendation of the President to the Board of Directors: Proposed Loan and Administration of Grant and Loan People's Republic of Bangladesh: Dhaka and Western Zone Transmission Grid Expansion Project.* Manila.
[b] ADB. 2019. *Technical Assistance to Mongolia for Methane Gas Supply Chain Development Master Plan.* Manila.
[c] ADB. 2019. *Technical Assistance for Preparing Sustainable Energy Projects in Central Asia.* Manila.
[d] ADB. 2019. *Technical Assistance to the Republic of Uzbekistan for Preparing Urban Development and Improvement Projects.* Manila.
[e] ADB. 2019. *Technical Assistance to the Islamic Republic of Pakistan for Preparing Urban Development Projects.* Manila.
[f] ADB. 2019. *Technical Assistance for Connecting the Railways of the Greater Mekong Subregion (Phase 2).* Manila.
[g] ADB. 2019. Regional: Developing Partnerships for Knowledge Sharing on Natural Capital Investment in the Yangtze River Economic Belt.
[h] ADB. 2019. *Technical Assistance for Strengthening Fiscal Governance and Sustainability in Public–Private Partnerships (Supplementary).* Manila.
[i] ADB. 2019. *Technical Assistance for Better Customs for Better Client Services in Central Asia Regional Economic Cooperation Countries.* Manila.
[j] ADB. 2019. *Technical Assistance for Developing an Accountability Mechanism Framework for Financial Intermediaries.* Manila.
Source: ADB database.

# Projects Funded by PRC Fund, 2005–2019

| Project Title | Project Number[a] | Dept | PRC Fund Approved Amount ($'000) | MOF PRC Approval Date | TA/Grant Approval Date[b] | Completion/ Expected Completion Date | Status | TCR Rating |
|---|---|---|---|---|---|---|---|---|
| **2005 Approvals** | | | **4,100** | | | | | |
| **Batch 1** | | | **2,300** | | | | | |
| 1 Support to Trade Facilitation and Capacity Building in the GMS | 6328-REG | SERD | 400 | 3-Jun-05 | 19-Jul-06 | 31-Dec-10 | Closed | S |
| 2 Development Study of the GMS Economic Corridors | 6310-REG | SERD | 400 | 3-Jun-05 | 20-Mar-06 | 14-Nov-12 | Closed | S |
| 3 Implementation of the Greater Mekong Subregion Cross-Border Transport Agreement | 6307-REG | SERD | 400 | 3-Jun-05 | 6-Mar-06 | 28-Apr-12 | Closed | S |
| 4 Enhancing the Business Environment in the GMS | 6266-REG | SERD | 200 | 3-Jun-05 | 31-Oct-05 | 28-Nov-08 | Closed | U |
| 5 Greater Mekong Subregion Phnom Penh Plan for Development Management Phase II (supplementary) | 6237-REG | SERD | 500 | 3-Jun-05 | 27-Jul-05 | 30-Apr-09 | Closed | S |
| 6 Capacity Building for Regional Cooperation in Central Asia | 6288-REG | CWRD | 400 | 3-Jun-05 | 16-Dec-05 | 28-Feb-09 | Closed | S |
| **Batch 2** | | | **1,800** | | | | | |
| 7 Partnership on Persistent Organic Pollutants Pesticides Management for Agricultural Production in Central Asian Countries | 6339-REG | CWRD | 400 | 22-Dec-05 | 25-Aug-06 | 16-Oct-08 | Closed | PS |
| 8 Technical Training and Capacity Building for Selected ASEAN+3 Countries on Regional Economic and Financial Monitoring | 6342-REG | ERCD | 500 | 22-Dec-05 | 21-Sep-06 | 31-Mar-11 | Closed | S |
| 9 Strengthening Carbon Financing for Regional Grassland Management in Northeast Asia | 7534-REG | EARD | 400 | 22-Dec-05 | 17-May-10 | 30-Sep-14 | Closed | S |
| 10 Expansion of Subregional Cooperation in Agriculture in the Greater Mekong Subregion | 6324-REG | SERD | 250 | 22-Dec-05 | 23-Jun-06 | 12-Oct-10 | Closed | S |
| 11 Support to Trade Facilitation and Capacity Building in the GMS[c] | 6328-REG | SERD | 250 | 22-Dec-05 | 19-Jul-06 | 31-Dec-10 | Closed | S |

| | Project Title | Project Number[a] | Dept | PRC Fund Approved Amount ($'000) | MOF PRC Approval Date | TA/Grant Approval Date[b] | Completion/ Expected Completion Date | Status | TCR Rating |
|---|---|---|---|---|---|---|---|---|---|
| | **2006 Approvals** | | | **2,970** | | | | | |
| | **Batch 1** | | | **1,670** | | | | | |
| 12 | Support Preparations for the CAREC Business Development Forum | 6340-REG | CWRD | 200 | 13-Jun-06 | 25-Aug-06 | 30-Apr-07 | Closed | S |
| 13 | Enhancement of Subregional Cooperation in BIMP-EAGA and IMT-GT | 6352-REG | SERD | 250 | 13-Jun-06 | 7-Nov-06 | 30-Nov-09 | Closed | S |
| 14 | Expansion of Subregional Cooperation in Agriculture in the Greater Mekong Subregion[d] | 6324-REG | SERD | 350 | 13-Jun-06 | 23-Jun-06 | 12-Oct-10 | Closed | S |
| 15 | Capacity Building for Designing, Negotiating and Implementing Free Trade Agreements in Selected Asian Developing Member Countries | 6345-REG | ERCD | 500 | 13-Jun-06 | 2-Oct-06 | 20-Sep-12 | Closed | S |
| 16 | ASEAN+3 Regional Guarantee and Investment Mechanism - Phase 2 | 6373-REG | ERCD | 300 | 13-Jun-06 | 17-Dec-06 | 27-Jun-11 | Closed | HS |
| 17 | Second ASEAN+3 Seminar on Poverty Reduction | 6382-REG | EARD | 70 | 13-Jun-06 | 15-Sep-06 | 30-Mar-07 | Closed | NR |
| | **Batch 2** | | | **1,300** | | | | | |
| 18 | Central Asia Regional Economic Cooperation: Capacity Development for Regional Cooperation in CAREC Participating Countries, Phase I | 6375-REG | CWRD | 500 | 1-Dec-06 | 18-Dec-06 | 30-Nov-10 | Closed | S |
| 19 | Transboundary Animal Disease Control for Poverty Reduction in the Greater Mekong Subregion | 6390-REG | SERD | 300 | 1-Dec-06 | 27-Mar-07 | 11-Oct-16 | Closed | PS |
| 20 | CAREC Members Electricity Regulators Forum | 6389-REG | CWRD | 500 | 1-Dec-06 | 26-Marc-07 | 17-Dec-09 | Closed | S |
| | **2007 Approvals** | | | **4,022** | | | | | |
| | **Batch 1** | | | **2,522** | | | | | |
| 21 | Strengthening Central Asia Regional Economic Cooperation, 2007–2011 | 6409-REG | CWRD | 500 | 2-Jul-07 | 27-Aug-07 | 31-Aug-13 | Closed | S |
| 22 | Capacity Building and Institutional Strengthening of the ASEAN Free Trade Area Units of Selected ASEAN Member Countries (Phase 1) | 6451-REG | ERCD | 500 | 2-Jul-07 | 28-Mar-08 | 30-Sep-14 | Closed | S |
| 23 | Enhancing the Development Effectiveness of the GMS Economic Cooperation Program (supplementary) | 6262-REG | SERD | 500 | 2-Jul-07 | 18-Sep-07 | 30-Jun-12 | Closed | S |
| 24 | GMS Core Environment Program and Biodiversity Conservation Corridors Initiative (Phase 1, supplementary) | 6289-REG | SERD | 500 | 2-Jul-07 | 11-Feb-08 | 31-Jan-16 | Closed | S |
| 25 | GMS Public Health Forum on Regional Cooperation in Communicable Disease Control and Health Systems Development (supplementary) | 6413-REG | SERD | 22 | 2-Jul-07 | 7-Nov-07 | 30-Apr-10 | Closed | HS |

| | Project Title | Project Number[a] | Dept | PRC Fund Approved Amount ($'000) | MOF PRC Approval Date | TA/Grant Approval Date[b] | Completion/ Expected Completion Date | Status | TCR Rating |
|---|---|---|---|---|---|---|---|---|---|
| 26 | Capacity Building for Monitoring and Evaluation in Participating Countries | 6410-REG | IED | 500 | 2-Jul-07 | 3-Sep-07 | 25-Nov-11 | Closed | S |
| | **Batch 2** | | | **1,500** | | | | | |
| 27 | Phnom Penh Plan for Development Management Phase III (supplementary) | 6407-REG | SERD | 500 | 16-Nov-07 | 7-Mar-08 | 31-Jan-12 | Closed | HS |
| 28 | Central Asia Regional Economic Cooperation Institute 2009–2012 | 6488-REG | CWRD | 500 | 16-Nov-07 | 24-Sep-08 | 25-Sep-15 | Closed | S |
| 29 | Supporting Boao Forum for Asia | 6444-REG | ERCD | 500 | 16-Nov-07 | 13-Feb-08 | 8-Mar-11 | Closed | S |
| **2008 Approvals** | | | | **4,250** | | | | | |
| | **Batch 1** | | | **2,250** | | | | | |
| 30 | Enhancing Transport and Trade Facilitation in the Greater Mekong Subregion | 6450-REG | SERD | 500 | 24-Jun-08 | 28-Mar-08 | 22-Dec-14 | Closed | S |
| 31 | Transboundary Animal Disease Control for Poverty Reduction in the Greater Mekong Subregion (supplementary)[e] | 6390-REG | SERD | 200 | 24-Jun-08 | 27-Feb-09 | 11-Oct-16 | Closed | PS |
| 32 | Small-scale Technical Assistance for Developing a Computable General Equilibrium Modeling Framework for Analyzing the Impacts of Power Trading Between Mongolia and the People's Republic of China | 6494-REG | EARD | 150 | 24-Jun-08 | 16-Oct-18 | 14-Sep-11 | Closed | S |
| 33 | Development Study of the GMS Economic Corridors (supplementary)[f] | 6310-REG | SERD | 400 | 24-Jun-08 | 7-July-08 | 14-Nov-12 | Closed | S |
| 34 | Regional Knowledge and Partnership Networks for Poverty Reduction and Inclusive Growth | 6502-REG | SDCC | 500 | 24-Jun-08 | 14-Nov-08 | 28-Oct-16 | Closed | PS |
| 35 | Capacity Development for National Economic Policy Analysis and Development Management, Phase III | 7226-CAM | SERD | 500 | 24-June-08 | 12-Jan-09 | 27-Nov-13 | Closed | S |
| | **Batch 2** | | | **2,000** | | | | | |
| 36 | Capacity Development for Monitoring and Evaluation | 7348-REG | IED | 500 | 17-Dec-08 | 17-Sep-09 | 31-Mar-06 | Closed | NR |
| 37 | Implementing the Greater Mekong Subregion Human Resource Development Strategy Framework and Action Plan 2009–2011 | 7275-REG | SERD | 500 | 17-Dec-08 | 29-Apr-09 | 12-Feb-14 | Closed | S |
| 38 | Accelerating the Implementation of the Core Agriculture Support Program | 6521-REG | SERD | 500 | 17-Dec-08 | 23-Dec-08 | 5-Jul-16 | Closed | S |
| 39 | Deposit Insurance Establishment | 7337-REG | EARD | 500 | 17-Dec-08 | 27-Aug-09 | 18-Mar-13 | Closed | S |
| **2009 Approvals** | | | | **2,000** | | | | | |
| | **Batch 1** | | | **1,000** | | | | | |
| 40 | Central Asia Regional Economic Cooperation: Working with the Private Sector in Trade Facilitation | 7353-REG | EARD | 500 | 31-May-09 | 25-Sep-09 | 31-Dec-15 | Closed | PS |

| | Project Title | Project Number[a] | Dept | PRC Fund Approved Amount ($'000) | MOF PRC Approval Date | TA/Grant Approval Date[b] | Completion/ Expected Completion Date | Status | TCR Rating |
|---|---|---|---|---|---|---|---|---|---|
| 41 | Asia Pacific Procurement Partnership Initiative | 7437-REG | PPFD | 500 | 31-May-09 | 11-Dec-09 | 25-Jul-17 | Closed | S |
| | **Batch 2** | | | **1,000** | | | | | |
| 42 | Strengthening Central Asia Regional Economic Cooperation, 2007–2011 (supplementary)[g] | 6409-REG | CWRD | 500 | 9-Dec-09 | 22-Feb-10 | 31-Aug-13 | Closed | S |
| 43 | GMS Phnom Penh Plan (PPP) for Development Management, Phase IV (supplementary) | 7431-REG | SERD | 500 | 9-Dec-09 | 5-Feb-10 | 31-Jul-13 | Closed | S |
| **2010 Approvals** | | | | **1,000** | | | | | |
| | **Special Batch** | | | **1,000** | | | | | |
| 44 | Supporting the Boao Forum for Asia in Regional Economic Integration and Partnership Dialogues | 7651-REG | OCO[h] | 500 | 6-May-10 | 22-Nov-10 | 30-Oct-15 | Closed | S |
| 45 | Strengthening the Coordination of the GMS Program | 7561-REG | SERD | 500 | 6-May-10 | 15-Jul-10 | 30-Apr-18 | Closed | S |
| **2011 Approvals** | | | | **1,300** | | | | | |
| | **Batch 1** | | | **500** | | | | | |
| 46 | Regional Program for Research and Capacity Development on Water Security | 7845-REG | SDCC | 500 | 15-Apr-11 | 12-Aug-11 | 20-Jan-16 | Closed | S |
| | **Batch 2** | | | **800** | | | | | |
| 47 | Poverty Reduction and Inclusive Growth Network in Asia Pacific (supplementary)[i] | 6502-REG | SDCC | 400 | 20-Nov-12 | 29-Apr-13 | 28-Oct-16 | Closed | PS |
| 48 | Support for Pan–Beibu Gulf Economic Cooperation[j] | 8017-REG | EARD | 400 | 20-Nov-12 | 13-Dec-11 | 31-Mar-16 | Closed | S |
| **2012 Approvals** | | | | **2,600** | | | | | |
| | **Batch 1** | | | **1,400** | | | | | |
| 49 | Provision of Knowledge Products and Services to DMCs through Systematic Knowledge | 8392-REG | ERCD | 500 | 20-Nov-12 | 30-May-13 | 1-Feb-19 | Closed | S |
| 50 | GMS Phnom Penh Plan for Development Management, Phase V (supplementary) | 8225-REG | SERD | 500 | 20-Nov-12 | 22-Jan-13 | 30-Oct-15 | Closed | HS |
| 51 | Supporting Capacity Development Needs of CAREC 2020 | 8301-REG | CWRD | 400 | 20-Nov-12 | 17-Dec-12 | 30-Jun-20 | Active | |
| | **Batch 2** | | | **1,200** | | | | | |
| 52 | Prevention and Control of HIV/AIDS and Other Communicable Diseases in Central Asia Regional Economic Cooperation Countries | 8367-REG | CWRD | 300 | 1-Mar-13 | 9-May-3 | 31-Dec-15 | Cancelled[k] | U |
| 53 | CAREC Trade Facilitation Program: Promoting Cooperation in Sanitary and Phytosanitary Measures | 8386-REG | EARD | 500 | 1-Marc-13 | 30-Jun-13 | 17-Dec-15 | Closed | HS |

| | Project Title | Project Number[a] | Dept | PRC Fund Approved Amount ($'000) | MOF PRC Approval Date | TA/Grant Approval Date[b] | Completion/ Expected Completion Date | Status | TCR Rating |
|---|---|---|---|---|---|---|---|---|---|
| 54 | Technical Training and Capacity Building for Selected Asian Countries on Regional Economic and Financial Monitoring – Phase II | 8433-REG | ERCD | 400 | 1-Mar-13 | 16-Aug-13 | 19-Feb-16 | Closed | S |
| **2013 Approvals** | | | | **3,325** | | | | | |
| | **Batch 1** | | | **2,100** | | | | | |
| 55 | South Asia Subregional Economic Cooperation Power System Expansion | 8412-NEP | SARD | 500 | 20-Jun-13 | 30-Jul-13 | 1-July-17 | Closed | NR |
| 56 | Second the GMS Corridor Towns Development Project | 8425-REG | SERD | 500 | 20-Jun-13 | 13-Aug-13 | 2-Nov-17 | Closed | NR |
| 57 | Promoting Regional Knowledge Sharing Partnerships | 8430-REG | EARD | 600 | 20-Jun-13 | 16-Aug-13 | 2-Apr-19 | Closed | S |
| 58 | Design of e-Governance Master Plan and Review of ICT Capacity in Academic Institutions | 8398-MYA | SDCC | 500 | 20-Jun-13 | 4-July-13 | 28-Dec-15 | Closed | HS |
| | **Batch 2** | | | **1,225** | | | | | |
| 59 | Developing Local Currency Bonds for Infrastructure Finance in ASEAN+3 | 8510-REG | SDCC | 225 | 13-Nov-13 | 21-Nov-13 | 29-Feb-16 | Closed | HS |
| 60 | Implementing the Greater Mekong Subregion Human Resource Development Strategy Framework and Action Plan Phase II | 8549-REG | SERD | 500 | 13-Nov-13 | 9-Dec-13 | 28-Sep-18 | Closed | PS |
| 61 | Asia-Pacific Community of Practice on Managing for Development Results – Strengthening Knowledge Partnerships on MfDR | 8636-REG | SDCC | 500 | 13-Nov-13 | 8-May-14 | 27-Jan-16 | Closed | S |
| **2014 Approvals** | | | | **3,800** | | | | | |
| | **Batch 1** | | | **1,500** | | | | | |
| 62 | Core Environment Program and Biodiversity Conservation Corridors Initiative in the GMS, Phase 2 (supplementary) | 7987-REG | SERD | 500 | 23-Jun-14 | 12-Dec-14 | 30-Jun-18 | Elapsed[i] | |
| 63 | Study for a Power Sector Financing Road Map within CAREC | 8727-REG | CWRD | 500 | 23-Jun-14 | 26-Sep-14 | 29-Mar-17 | Closed | S |
| 64 | CAREC: Working with the Private Sector in Trade Facilitation (Phase 2) | 8746-REG | EARD | 500 | 23-Jun-14 | 30-Oct-14 | 20-Oct-19 | Closed | NR |
| | **Batch 2** | | | **2,300** | | | | | |
| 65 | CAREC Knowledge Sharing and Services in Transport and Transport Facilitation | 8789-REG | CWRD | 400 | 10-Dec-14 | 12-Dec-14 | 31-Jul-19 | Closed | NR |
| 66 | Harmonizing the GMS Power Systems to Facilitate Regional Power Trade | 8830-REG | SERD | 500 | 10-Dec-14 | 16-Dec-14 | 31-Dec-19 | Active | |
| 67 | Infrastructure Public–Private Partnership Pipeline Development Support | 8908-REG | OPPP | 750 | 10-Dec-14 | 23-Jun-15 | 1-Aug-19 | Active | |

| | Project Title | Project Number[i] | Dept | PRC Fund Approved Amount ($'000) | MOF PRC Approval Date | TA/Grant Approval Date[b] | Completion/ Expected Completion Date | Status | TCR Rating |
|---|---|---|---|---|---|---|---|---|---|
| 68 | Building Capacity for Enhanced Connectivity in Southeast Asia (supplementary) | 8836-REG | SERD | 250 | 10-Dec-14 | 28-May-15 | 29-Mar-19 | Closed | HS |
| 69 | Greater Mekong Subregion: Capacity Development for Economic Zones in Border Areas | 8989-REG | SERD | 400 | 10-Dec-14 | 12-Nov-15 | 4-Apr-19 | Closed | S |
| **2015 Approvals** | | | | **4,025** | | | | | |
| | **Batch 1** | | | **1,225** | | | | | |
| 70 | Strategy for Northeast Asia Power System Interconnection | 9001-MON | EARD | 500 | 23-Jul-15 | 27-Nov-15 | 15-Aug-19 | Active | |
| 71 | Supporting the Asian Exim Banks Forum | 8973-REG | OCO[m] | 500 | 23-Jul-15 | 5-Oct-15 | 4-Oct-20 | Active | |
| 72 | Provision of Knowledge Products and Services to Developing Member Countries through Systematic Knowledge Sharing (supplementary)[n] | 8392-REG | ERCD | 225 | 23-Jul-15 | 3-Nov-15 | 1-Feb-19 | Closed | S |
| | **Batch 2** | | | **2,800** | | | | | |
| 73 | Universal Health Coverage for Inclusive Growth: Supporting the Implementation of the Operational Plan for Health 2015–2020 (supplementary) | 8983-REG | SDCC | 500 | 6-Jan-16 | 31-Aug-16 | 31-Dec-20 | Active | |
| 74 | Capturing the Opportunities and Addressing the Risks (supplementary) | 8978-KGZ | CWRD | 200 | 6-Jan-16 | 17-Nov-16 | 31-Dec-19 | Active | |
| 75 | Promoting Regional Knowledge Sharing Partnerships (supplementary)[o] | 8430-REG | EARD | 500 | 6-Jan-16 | 21-Nov-16 | 31-Dec-18 | Closed | S |
| 76 | Regional Evaluation Capacity Development II | 9118-REG | IED | 500 | 6-Jan-16 | 18-May-16 | 31-Dec-19 | Active | |
| 77 | Connecting the Railways of the Greater Mekong Subregion | 9123-REG | SERD | 500 | 6-Jan-16 | 21-Jun-16 | 12-Dec-18 | Closed | S |
| 78 | Support for Project Implementation of the Nepal Earthquake Rehabilitation and Reconstruction Program (supplementary) | 8910-NEP | SARD | 600 | 6-Jan-16 | 4-Mar-16 | 31-Dec-19 | Active | |
| **2016 Approvals** | | | | **4,950** | | | | | |
| | **Batch 1** | | | **3,750** | | | | | |
| 79 | Strengthening Water Security in the Aral Sea Basin | TBD | CWRD | 500 | 11-Jul-16 | TBD | TBD | Elapsed[p] | |
| 80 | Policy Coordination and Planning of Border Economic Zones of the PRC and Viet Nam | 9293-REG | EARD | 400 | 11-Jul-16 | 10-Jan-17 | 29-Mar-019 | Closed | NR |
| 81 | Energy Supply Improvement Investment Program (Tranche 2) | 0523-AFG | CWRD | 1,000 | 11-Jul-16 | 16-Dec-16 | 30-Jun-23 | Active | |
| 82 | Strengthening Knowledge Management in Central and West Asia (supplementary) | 8936-REG | CWRD | 650 | 11-Jul-16 | 18-Nov-16 | 15-Mar-19 | Closed | NR |

| | Project Title | Project Number[a] | Dept | PRC Fund Approved Amount ($'000) | MOF PRC Approval Date | TA/Grant Approval Date[b] | Completion/ Expected Completion Date | Status | TCR Rating |
|---|---|---|---|---|---|---|---|---|---|
| 83 | Advancing RCI through BIMP-EAGA and IMT-GT (supplementary) | 8814-REG | SERD | 700 | 11-Jul-16 | 31-Aug-16 | 6-Feb-19 | Closed | S |
| 84 | Central Asia Regional Economic Cooperation: Supporting Capacity Development Needs of CAREC 2020 (supplementary)[q] | 8301-REG | CWRD | 500 | 25-Oct-16 | 8-Dec-16 | 30-Jun-20 | Active | |
| | **Batch 2** | | | **1,200** | | | | | |
| 85 | Promoting Green Local Currency Denominated Bonds for Infrastructure Development ASEAN+3 | 9294-REG | ERCD | 500 | 27-Dec-16 | 24-Jan-17 | 30-Jun-19 | Closed | HS |
| 86 | Promoting Low Carbon Development in CAREC Program Cities | 9308-REG | EARD | 700 | 27-Dec-16 | 6-Apr-17 | 31-Dec-19 | Active | |
| | **2017 Approvals** | | | **5,150** | | | | | |
| | **Batch 1** | | | **5,150** | | | | | |
| 87 | Revitalizing the Ecosystem of Ravi River Basin | 9463-PAK | CWRD | 550 | 8-Dec-17 | 12-Dec-17 | 30-Sep-19 | Active | |
| 88 | Water and Sanitation Strategy Development and Capacity Building | 9481-UZB | CWRD | 800 | 8-Dec-17 | 21-Dec-17 | 28-Feb-21 | Active | |
| 89 | Enhancing Regional Knowledge Sharing Partnership | 9531-REG | EARD | 750 | 8-Dec-17 | 15-Jun-18 | 31-Jul-21 | Active | |
| 90 | Modernizing Sanitary and Phytosanitary Measures to Facilitate Trade | 9500-REG | EARD | 800 | 8-Dec-17 | 13-Feb-18 | 30-Sep-20 | Active | |
| 91 | Capacity Building Support for Asia–Pacific Economic Cooperation Financial Regulators Training | 9501-REG | ERCD | 600 | 8-Dec-17 | 12-Feb-18 | 31-Dec-19 | Active | |
| 92 | Strengthening Asia's Financial Safety Nets and Resolution Mechanisms | 9497-REG | ERCD | 125 | 8-Dec-17 | 29-Jan-18 | 31-Dec-20 | Active | |
| 93 | Strengthening Compliance Review and Accountability to Project Affected Persons of Financial Intermediaries | 9466-REG | OCRP | 225 | 8-Dec-17 | 14-Dec-17 | 4-Feb-19 | Closed | S |
| 94 | Water Supply Scheme for Tete Settlement | 0638-PNG | PARD | 800 | 8-Dec-17 | 21-Feb-19 | 30-Jun-21 | Active | |
| 95 | Strengthening Institutions for Localizing Agenda 2030 for Sustainable Development (supplementary) | 9387-REG | SDCC | 500 | 8-Dec-17 | 23-Mar-18 | 31-Dec-20 | Active | |
| | **2018 Approvals** | | | **6,575** | | | | | |
| | **Batch 1** | | | **2,800** | | | | | |
| 96 | Enhancing Effectiveness of Subregional Programs to Advance Regional Cooperation and Integration in Southeast Asia | 9572-REG | SERD | 700 | 28-Jun-18 | 22-Aug-18 | 31-Dec-20 | Active | |
| 97 | Knowledge Solutions for Inclusive and Sustainable Development | 9602-BAN | SARD | 500 | 28-Jun-18 | 1-Oct-18 | 31-Aug-21 | Active | |

| | Project Title | Project Number[a] | Dept | PRC Fund Approved Amount ($'000) | MOF PRC Approval Date | TA/Grant Approval Date[b] | Completion/ Expected Completion Date | Status | TCR Rating |
|---|---|---|---|---|---|---|---|---|---|
| 98 | Strengthening Knowledge and Actions for Air Quality Improvement | 9608-REG | SDCC | 800 | 28-Jun-18 | 5-Oct-18 | 30-Sep-21 | Active | |
| 99 | Implementing Integrated Trade Agenda in Central Asia Regional Economic Cooperation Program | 9712-REG | EARD | 800 | 28-Jun-18 | 15-Feb-19 | 30-Jun-21 | Active | |
| | **Batch 2** | | | **2,800** | | | | | |
| 100 | Assessing Economic Corridor Development Potential Among Kazakhstan, Uzbekistan, and Tajikistan | 9630-REG | CWRD | 800 | 9-Oct-18 | 31-Oct-18 | 31-Dec-20 | Active | |
| 101 | Railway Sector Development in Central Asian Regional Economic Cooperation Countries | 9641-REG | CWRD | 1,000 | 9-Oct-18 | 14-Nov-18 | 31-Dec-22 | Active | |
| 102 | Integrated High Impact Innovation in Sustainable Energy Technology | 9690-REG | SDCC | 1,000 | 9-Oct-18 | 13-Dec-18 | 30-Sep-23 | Active | |
| | **Batch 3** | | | **975** | | | | | |
| 103 | Developing an Accountability Mechanism Framework for Financial Intermediaries[r] | 9718-REG | OCRP | 225 | 4-Mar-16 | 7-Mar-16 | 8-Feb-20 | Closed | S |
| 104 | Dhaka and Western Zone Transmission Grid Expansion Project[r] | 0675-BAN | SARD | 750 | 1-Mar-19 | 11-Dec-19 | 31-Dec-24 | Active | |
| **2019 Approvals** | | | | **8,075** | | | | | |
| | **Batch 1** | | | **3,600** | | | | | |
| 105 | Better Customs for Better Client Services in Central Asia Regional Economic Cooperation Countries | 9824-REG | EARD | 500 | 8-Jul-19 | 14-Oct-19 | 30-Sep-21 | Active | |
| 106 | Methane Gas Supply Chain Development Master Plan | 9938-MON | EARD | 500 | 8-Jul-19 | 25-Jan-20 | 31-Jan-22 | Active | |
| 107 | Preparing Urban Development and Improvement Projects | 9715-UZB | CWRD | 1,000 | 8-Jul-19 | 31-Oct-19 | 31-Dec-23 | Active | |
| 108 | Preparing Sustainable Energy Projects in Central Asia | 9792-REG | CWRD | 1,600 | 8-Jul-19 | 8-Aug-19 | 31-Dec-20 | Active | |
| | **Batch 2** | | | **2,725** | | | | | |
| 109 | Preparing Urban Development Projects | 9839-PAK | CWRD | 1,500 | 13-Oct-19 | TBD | 31-Dec-21 | Active | |
| 110 | Strengthening Fiscal Governance and Sustainability in Public–Private Partnerships | 9791-REG | SDCC | 500 | 13-Oct-19 | 12-Nov-19 | 31-Dec-22 | Active | |
| 111 | Connecting the Railways of the Greater Mekong Subregion (Phase 2) | 9918-REG | SERD | 500 | 13-Oct-19 | 19-Dec-19 | 31-Dec-21 | Active | |
| 112 | Developing Partnerships for Knowledge Sharing on Natural Capital Investment in the Yangtze River Economic Belt | 9846-REG | EARD | 225 | 13-Oct-19 | 15-Oct-19 | 31-Dec-20 | Active | |

| | Project Title | Project Number[a] | Dept | PRC Fund Approved Amount ($'000) | MOF PRC Approval Date | TA/Grant Approval Date[b] | Completion/ Expected Completion Date | Status | TCR Rating |
|---|---|---|---|---|---|---|---|---|---|
| | **Batch 3** | | | **1,750** | | | | | |
| 113 | Greater Mekong Subregion Sustainable Agriculture and Food Security Program | 9916-REG | SERD | 750 | 9-Jan-20 | 18-Dec-19 | 31-Mar-25 | Active | |
| 114 | Creating Ecosystems for Green Local Currency Bonds for Infrastructure Development in ASEAN+3 | 9953-REG | ERCD | 500 | 9-Jan-20 | 4-Mar-20 | 28-Feb-22 | Active | |
| 115 | Strengthening Social Protection in the Pacific | 9963-REG | PARD | 500 | 9-Jan-20 | 15-Apr-20 | 31-Mar-25 | Active | |
| | **Total Committed Funds** | | | **58,142** | | | | | |
| | **Total PRC Commitment[s]** | | | **76,000** | | | | | |
| | **Balance** | | | **17,858** | | | | | |

ADB = Asian Development Bank; ASEAN = Association of Southeast Asian Nations; ASEAN+3 = ASEAN plus Japan, People's Republic of China, and Republic of Korea; BAN = Bangladesh; BIMP- EAGA = Brunei Darussalam–Indonesia–Malaysia–Philippines–East Asian Growth Area; CAREC = Central Asia Regional Economic Cooperation; CWRD = Central and West Asia Department; CAM = Cambodia; Dept = department; DMC = developing member country; EARD = East Asia Department; ERCD = Economic Research and Regional Cooperation Department; FP = for processing; GMS = Greater Mekong Subregion; HS = highly successful; ICT = information and communication technology; IED = Independent Evaluation Department; IMT-GT = Indonesia–Malaysia Third Growth Triangle; MfDR = Managing for Development Results; MOF = Ministry of Finance, PRC; MON = Mongolia; MYA = Myanmar; NEP = Nepal; PAK = Pakistan; PARD = Pacific Department; PPFD = Procurement, Portfolio and Financial Management Department; PPP = public–private partnership, PRC = People's Republic of China; PRC Fund = People's Republic of China Poverty Reduction and Regional Cooperation Fund; RCI = regional cooperation and integration; REG = regional; S = successful; SARD = South Asia Department; SDCC = Sustainable Development and Climate Change Department; SERD = Southeast Asia Department; TA = technical assistance; TBD = to be determined; TCR = technical assistance completion report; U = unsuccessful; UZB = Uzbekistan.

a   Project numbers in italics denote projects cofinanced either by ADB or other partners.
b   The TA approval date and the expected completion date were updated on 31 March 2019 with information from the ADB database.
c   Additional funding before ADB project approval for TA 6328-REG.
d   Additional funding before ADB project approval for TA 6324-REG.
e   Additional funding approval for TA 6390-REG.
f   Additional funding approval for TA 6310-REG.
g   Additional funding approval for TA 6409-REG.
h   Following its realignment in April 2019, the Office of Cofinancing Operations (OCO) ceased to exist. The administration of the PRC Fund was transferred to a new Partner Funds Division (SDPF) under SDCC.
i   Additional funding approval for TA 6502-REG.
j   Includes partial cancellation of $100,000 made on 4 July 2014.
k   Funding allocation was returned to the fund pool as the TA was cancelled due to consultant recruitment issues and was closed in September 2014.
l   Funding allocation was returned to the fund pool as the 6-month period for ADB approval after PRC MOF had elapsed, as stated in Fund Implementation Guidelines (Section 6).
m   Following the realignment of the Office of Cofinancing Operations (OCO) in April 2019, OCO ceased to exist. The administration of the PRC Fund was transferred to a new Partner Funds Division (SDPF) under SDCC.
n   Additional funding approval for TA 8392-REG.
o   Additional funding approval for TA 8430-REG.
p   Funding allocation was returned to the fund pool as the 6-month period for ADB approval after PRC MOF had elapsed, as stated in Fund Implementation Guidelines (Section 6). The TA did not proceed to ADB approval.
q   Additional funding approval for TA 8301-REG.
r   Approved by PRC MOF in March 2019.
s   Excludes the $1 million provided to the ADB Institute.
Source: ADB database.

www.ingramcontent.com/pod-product-compliance
Lightning Source LLC
Chambersburg PA
CBHW041122280326
41928CB00061B/3488